Generations Z and Alpha Students at the Piano

Generations Z and Alpha Students at the Piano

A GUIDE FOR PIANO TEACHERS

Diana Dumlavwalla
Melody Morrison

BLOOMSBURY ACADEMIC
NEW YORK • LONDON • OXFORD • NEW DELHI • SYDNEY

BLOOMSBURY ACADEMIC

Bloomsbury Publishing Inc, 1359 Broadway, New York, NY 10018, USA
Bloomsbury Publishing Plc, 50 Bedford Square, London, WC1B 3DP, UK
Bloomsbury Publishing Ireland, 29 Earlsfort Terrace, Dublin 2, D02 AY28, Ireland

BLOOMSBURY, BLOOMSBURY ACADEMIC and the Diana logo are trademarks of Bloomsbury Publishing Plc

First published in the United States of America 2026

Copyright © Diana Dumlavwalla and Melody Morrison, 2026

For legal purposes the constitute an extension of this copyright page.

Cover design: Sally Rinehart
Cover image © FatCamera/Getty Images

All rights reserved. No part of this publication may be: i) reproduced or transmitted in any form, electronic or mechanical, including photocopying, recording or by means of any information storage or retrieval system without prior permission in writing from the publishers; or ii) used or reproduced in any way for the training, development or operation of artificial intelligence (AI) technologies, including generative AI technologies. The rights holders expressly reserve this publication from the text and data mining exception as per Article 4(3) of the Digital Single Market Directive (EU) 2019/790.

Bloomsbury Publishing Inc does not have any control over, or responsibility for, any third-party websites referred to or in this book. All internet addresses given in this book were correct at the time of going to press. The author and publisher regret any inconvenience caused if addresses have changed or sites have ceased to exist, but can accept no responsibility for any such changes.

Library of Congress Cataloging-in-Publication Data
Names: Dumlavwalla, Diana author | Morrison, Melody author
Title: Generations Z and Alpha students at the piano : a guide for piano teachers / Diana Dumlavwalla and Melody Morrison.
Description: New York : Bloomsbury Academic, 2026. | Includes bibliographical references and index.
Identifiers: LCCN 2025035896 (print) | LCCN 2025035897 (ebook) | ISBN 9798881805289 hardback | ISBN 9798881805296 paperback | ISBN 9798881867898 pdf | ISBN 9798881805302 epub
Subjects: LCSH: Piano—Instruction and study | Generation Z—Education | Generation Alpha—Education | Music—Instruction and study—Technological innovations
Classification: LCC MT220 .D87 2026 (print) | LCC MT220 (ebook) | DDC 786.2071—dc23/eng/20251202
LC record available at https://lccn.loc.gov/2025035896
LC ebook record available at https://lccn.loc.gov/2025035897

ISBN: HB: 979-8-8818-0528-9
PB: 979-8-8818-0529-6
ePDF: 979-8-8818-6789-8
ePub: 979-8-8818-0530-2

Typeset by Amnet
Printed and bound in the United States of America

For product safety related questions contact productsafety@bloomsbury.com.

To find out more about our authors and books visit www.bloomsbury.com and sign up for our newsletters.

Contents

List of Figures vi
List of Tables vii
Preface viii
Acknowledgments xi

1　A Product of the Past? 1
2　What's in a Generation? 25
3　Getting to Know Them: Understanding Generation Z 43
4　Mapping Their World: Who Is Generation Alpha? 57
5　Striking the Right Chord: Addressing Generations Z and Alpha Challenges and Strengths in Piano Teaching 75
6　Fostering Creativity 99
7　Understanding Their Musical Tastes 113
8　A Peek into the Studio of Today 123
9　Proven Strategies You Can Use 145

Index 173

Figures

1.1	Chiroplast, front view	3
1.2	Chiroplast, back view	4
1.3	Clavier à Lampe (automatic electrical musical instrument)	13
1.4	Gameplay from the CD-ROM *Jumpstart Music* (1998), showing the Rhythm Game	14
1.5	AMT's Computer Connection column	15
1.6	The internet age	16
2.1	Characteristics of the Greatest Generation	29
2.2	Characteristics of the Silent Generation	31
2.3	Characteristics of the baby boomers	33
2.4	Characteristics of Gen X	36
2.5	Characteristics of the millennials	39
3.1	Gen Z technology and influential events	45
5.1	Sample progress map for Christian Petzold's Minuet in G	78
6.1	The interrelation of technology, music making at the piano, and other art forms within creative expression	103
6.2	Three gaming categories	109
7.1	Inverted U diagram showing relationship between student interest and music difficulty	115
9.1	Concept map of topics based on Wakulla Springs	148
9.2	Emojis on a student's piece to convey moods	157
9.3	Proper hand position at the piano	160
9.4	Do-re-mi ladder	165
9.5	Idea board for Chopin's Nocturne in E Minor	167
9.6	Composing based on emojis	169
9.7	USB-B–to–USB-A cord	171

Tables

4.1	Core Technologies Defining the Gen Alpha Experience	61
6.1	Characteristics of the Creative Personality	101
9.1	Music Instructional Apps	153
9.2	Backing-Track Resources	154
9.3	Tools for Exposing Students to a Wide Range of Musical Styles	158
9.4	Digital Tools for Compositions and Arrangements	161
9.5	Elements of Sara Mullett's Animal Actions Rhythm Game	166
9.6	Compositional Tools for Young Students	170
9.7	DAW-Inspired Tools	170

Preface

The bedrock of any comprehensive teaching philosophy is understanding who you are teaching. Just as teachers regularly assign their students homework, teachers in turn must do their own homework in order to provide effective instruction, learning as much as they can about the individuals they have been charged to guide through the subject matter at hand. This is especially important when working with students who are younger and where a significant generational gap is evident.

Colloquially, previous generations have seen youth as the promise for the future, full of fresh energy, and willing to try new things. In a negative light, young people are sometimes seen as disrespectful, willing to forgo sacred traditions, and perhaps even lazy. Older generations are often shocked at the popular culture embraced by youth. Take, for example, Elvis Presley. In the 1950s, his dance moves were considered provocative and controversial. Young people of the time could not get enough of his hip shaking and gyrations, but it also caused great anger and criticism. Eventually, Elvis's moves became iconic and mainstream, leading to his worldwide fame and overall influence in popular music. In the 1960s and 1970s, the counterculture movement, which championed defiance to the establishment, sparked a sweeping social, cultural, and political movement across the Western world and shocked the same adults who were fawning over Elvis just twenty years earlier. The rise of rap and hip-hop in the 1980s and 1990s, often with explicit lyrics and themes, stunned those who were touting peace and love with the hippie movement just a few decades earlier. Nowadays, social media and its impact on society have many of the older generations scratching their heads. You get the drift—older generations will always be shocked and shaken by those who come after them.

Currently, the focus is on Generations Z and Alpha, the cohort of young people flooding our K–12 schools and colleges and universities. Like those who have come before them, they bring their unique preferences, culture, and youthful rebellious spirit. Those educating our youth need to become familiar with their characteristics. However, there is something unique about these generations that we have not seen before. Generations Z and Alpha have been immersed in technology and the internet from a very young age, often from birth. These generations do not remember a time when accessing all information at any given moment was not at their fingertips. They have been raised with screens and devices of all sizes, including cell phones, tablets, laptops, TVs—technology that has served as sources of entertainment, communication, and education. Not since the industrial revolution have we seen such a drastic change in the way our society operates. Furthermore, the incessant use of technology is not changing just how we do things. Research shows that it is altering the way brains function, affecting such areas as cognitive development and the sleep cycle. Such digital activities as gaming and social media have led to new discoveries in reward systems that are highly engaging. The infiltration of technology into our society is a significant influence on Generations Z and Alpha and has brought about distinctive characteristics and challenges for these cohorts. Educators need to be aware of these issues in order to connect with these generations in meaningful ways.

Traditionally and perhaps stereotypically, the private piano lesson can be seen as an intensive, highly concentrated session that focuses on what some people see as stuffy classical music. Typically, the master-apprentice approach establishes the structure for this type of educational setting. This is where one student is the sole focus of the teacher for a given amount of time and receives customized, one-on-one instruction on repertoire, technique, and artistic development. This can lead to many benefits and many challenges. A power dynamic where the teacher is the ultimate authority on the subject matter can arise from this situation. The conventional content usually covered in a traditional piano lesson can sometimes seem outdated, old-fashioned, and just plain boring in our modern world. To attract and retain the young students of today, it is important to communicate with them in ways that are less authoritative and keep them engaged and interested in piano lessons by building on the traditions of the past while using updated strategies and tools from our modern era.

We came to this realization as we prepared to submit proposals for the 2023 National Conference on Keyboard Pedagogy and the 2024 Music Teachers National Association Conference. With the distinctive features of Generations Z and Alpha often dominating news cycles, blogs, and opinion pieces, we realized it was time to figure out how this works with piano lessons. We aren't the first to acknowledge this. However, we felt that our specific lines of expertise could create a new perspective on how piano instructors could adjust and refine their pedagogical approaches. When we were approached to write this book, it felt like a natural next step.

While our goal for this publication is to provide a comprehensive compendium for teaching the piano to Generations Z and Alpha students, we acknowledge that trends and technology are constantly evolving. We hope to debunk some commonly held stereotypes about these cohorts of young people, identify their unique characteristics, reflect on the challenges they face, and critically examine how world events have shaped their lives.

In chapter 1, we look in the rearview mirror to see how historical developments in pedagogy and technology influence what we do as teachers today. Chapter 2 looks at what defines a generation and provides an overview of the last five generations. The defining characteristics and experiences of Generations Z and Alpha are examined in chapters 3 and 4. In chapter 5, we identify some of the specific strengths and challenges associated with individuals from these generations. This insight can help teachers to customize lessons for their students' individual preferences. Then, the importance of creativity and how to foster it is discussed in chapter 6. Understanding the musical tastes of our students, as explored in chapter 7, is another key perspective to address as teachers dive deeper into their role as piano instructors. In chapter 8, we hear directly from active teachers working "in the trenches" and creating effective solutions as they adapt their pedagogical strategies for the current younger generations. Finally, chapter 9 serves as a resource for specific strategies and tools you can use with your students in the studio.

As we crafted this book, we studied existing literature to give us an informed understanding of generational research, along with the historical developments of piano pedagogy and technology. We also examined conceptual psychology research, as well as educational research to break down some of the mystique behind understanding creativity and musical taste. Lastly, interviews were conducted with seven teachers to obtain firsthand knowledge regarding how they successfully work with Generations Z and Alpha students in today's modern studio. With this information in hand, we hope to shed light on how these developments influence learning preferences of the current young student population, specifically in piano education, and how instructors can find ways to embrace these attributes in their lesson planning. Our purpose is to approach this topic with an open mind and compassion.

Acknowledgments

A publication of this scope is a first for both of us, and there are many people we would like to thank for their direct and indirect contributions to this project.

We are deeply grateful to all our teachers and students who have inspired us in countless ways. Our teachers first introduced us to the meaning of true musical artistry and served as timeless examples of pedagogical excellence. Our experiences with students strengthened our ability to adapt, think creatively, and honor different learning needs.

The team at Bloomsbury has been outstanding, and we sincerely appreciate their professionalism. An enormous thank you to our acquisition editor, Michael Tan, who first approached us at the 2024 MTNA Conference in Atlanta to inquire if we would be interested in writing a book on this topic. His sound advice, prompt responses, and genuine encouragement helped us stay on schedule and ultimately launch this publication at the 2026 MTNA Conference in Chicago. We also extend our gratitude to Niki Guinan, our copy editor, for her thorough and detailed review of our work. We greatly appreciate Della Vache, our production editor, who ensured the successful completion of this book. We are indebted to the anonymous peer reviewers who examined our proposal and provided essential feedback before we began writing the manuscript.

Learning from colleagues in the field who make a difference in young people's lives was invaluable as we wrote this book. Thank you to Penny Lazarus, Leila Viss, Chee-Hwa Tan, Marie Lee, Joe Harkins, Pilar Plazas, and Ashley Danyew for generously sharing their insights for this publication.

We owe heartfelt appreciation to Pamela Pike, Melody Ng, and Tony Caramia, who generously devoted their precious time to provide the final reviews of our manuscript.

Finally, we are extremely indebted to our families, especially our parents, for all the love, support, and guidance they have given us throughout our lives. We would not be where we are today without them. Lastly, faith is a central part of each of our lives, and we are eternally thankful to God for all the gifts bestowed upon us.

1 A Product of the Past?

At the dawn of the new millennium, a two-part article series was published in *American Music Teacher*, one of the leading journal publications aimed at independent music teachers. The authors begin with a quote from a speech delivered by Carolyn Bowen at the 1927 Music Teachers National Association Conference:

> *The child of long, long ago with the . . . Richardson's "Instruction Book"—practising with pennies on her hands, and tears in her eyes—counting 1-a-a-and to something she didn't understand,—working on material usually titled "Lesson I" or "Lesson II," translating As and Bs on the staff to As and Bs on the piano,—learning scales from signatures,—spelling chords laboriously—reading a language she had no knowledge of—using a technique based on the old harpsichord,—if it had a base; I say that child belongs to the past, that child is only a memory.*[1]

It is quite astounding to think that this quote is from a century ago. From this description, we can hear the moans and grumbles of students who protest taking piano lessons. The last quarter-century since this was written has certainly seen an increase in teaching strategies and tools meant to engage students meaningfully at the piano. It is safe to say that at least a segment of today's piano-teaching field frowns upon a teaching approach that favors a dry, unmusical method—one only focused on the memorization of abstract symbols and metronomic playing. This teaching philosophy usually stems from teachers who use only approaches familiar to them during their student days and who don't engage in continuing education and further development. It is also a product of when we don't necessarily learn from our field's past triumphs and failures. As we enter a discussion of how we can best serve our dynamic and ever-evolving students, let us take a look at past teaching trends, how they have developed over time, and how they have led us to where we are today.

A Historical Tour of the Development of Piano Teaching

The approach to playing the piano has evolved over the centuries, mainly due to the various keyboard instruments that served as the precursors to our modern-day instrument, the pianoforte. Because the physical characteristics of earlier instruments, like the harpsichord, clavichord, and fortepiano, are different, pianists employed different playing techniques. The plethora of treatises and methods written by pedagogues and performing keyboardists, along with written accounts from piano students, provide historians with ample evidence to trace the historical development of common piano-teaching practices. This summary is based on the writings of Reginald Gerig (*Famous Pianists and Their Techniques*, 2007) and Stewart Gordon (*The Well-Tempered Keyboard Teacher*, 2000). Their publications are held in high regard among piano educators and serve as key resources for tracing the historical evolution of piano-teaching philosophies.

During the baroque period in the seventeenth and early eighteenth centuries, finger action was the focus of piano technique. Treatises by Diruta, Couperin, and Rameau advocate for a hand that is level with the arm and wrist, with the fingers arched. The most influential pedagogical writing of the late eighteenth and early nineteenth centuries is the "Essay on the True Art of Playing Keyboard Instruments" (1762) by C. P. E. Bach. He endorses arched fingers, relaxed muscles, and the inclusion of the thumb as a playing unit. It is important to note that Bach attempts to emphasize the fact that musical and expressive interpretation should be a priority, alongside well-executed skill. His treatise is also highly regarded as an excellent resource for keyboard embellishments. The skill of improvisation, particularly with the use of ornamentation and figured bass, was also highly valued during this time.

Moving into the Classical era, the attention focused on achieving an elegant sound, lightness of touch, and musical sensitivity. Johann Nepomuk Hummel's treatise "Art of Playing the Pianoforte" (1827) espouses these values and offers teachers what were, at the time, forward-thinking ideas, including encouraging students to keep their eyes trained on the score and not letting them play too fast. He advocates for limited physical movement at the instrument to help achieve the desired grace and finesse.

It was around this time that mechanical teaching aids started appearing and were seen as ways to achieve higher levels of technical proficiency faster.

The most widely used device was the chiroplast, invented by Johann Bernard Logier (see figures 1.1 and 1.2). A rather oppressive-looking device, the chiroplast was intended to train hands into the proper playing position.

Friedrich Kalkbrenner created a less-confining device that had rails where the pianist's wrists and partial forearms would rest while playing the piano. Today, many of us would gawk at these contraptions to enhance a pianist's technique. However, by the mid-nineteenth century, significant interest among some pianists was mounting regarding the mechanical aspects of their craft. This led to the creation of exercises and études to bolster finger strength and action but with less attention to sound quality.

High-level virtuosity was a necessary attribute of pianists in the romantic period, and Franz Liszt is often associated with this dramatic turn on the concert stage. He received his early instruction from his father, who followed Czerny's regimen as a guiding framework: two hours of scales and études with a metronome, one hour of sight-reading, and the remaining time devoted to composing.

At the age of sixteen, Liszt himself started his highly successful teaching practice. He began offering instruction in the typical setting of one-to-one lessons. However, in the last quarter of his life, he conducted more of his teaching in the master class setting, as it was his preference. Students

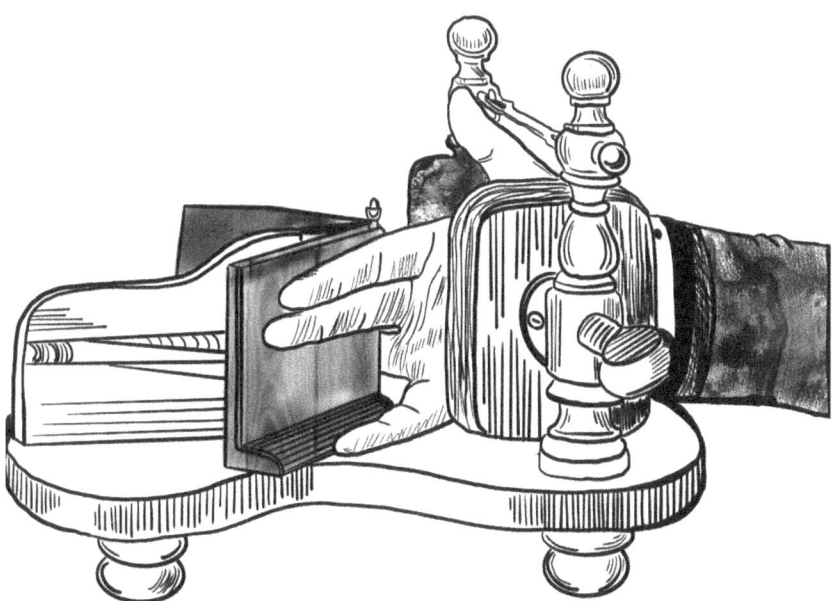

Figure 1.1 Chiroplast, front view. *Illustration by the author.*

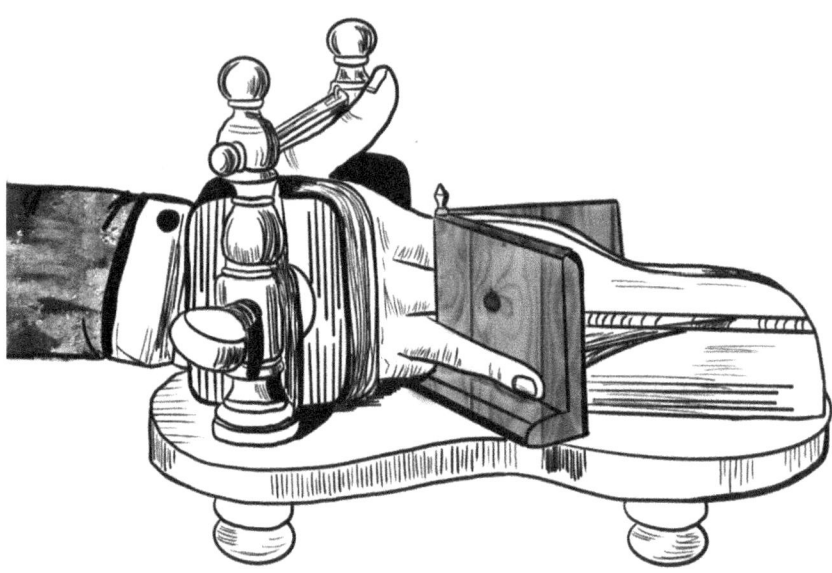

Figure 1.2 Chiroplast, back view. *Illustration by the author.*

gathered in groups not just to play for him, the master teacher, and learn from his advice. They also gained much knowledge by observing him work with other pianists. Students chose what to play and when they were ready to play. The master class setting continues to be an enduring aspect of piano education, particularly at the higher levels in conservatories and postsecondary institutions. The dynamics of being with other pianists and learning from one another in a group setting have yielded many benefits.

In terms of his physical approach to the piano, Liszt recommended sitting slightly higher than what pianists of the time were typically used to. He also encouraged students to use the fleshy part of the finger to help with the quality of tone. This contrasts with the highly arched fingers favored earlier. The concept of weight technique was espoused by teachers like Rudolf Maria Breithaupt (1873–1945), whose written material provides detailed explanations of his approach.

The mid- to late nineteenth century also saw the rise of the nationalist schools of playing, particularly the Russian, English, and French schools. Specifically, the teaching approaches of the Russian and French schools reflected and complemented the repertoire written in their respective countries.

Russian School

The influence of piano pedagogy from the St. Petersburg and Moscow Conservatories has become deeply embedded in the global tradition of piano instruction. The development of sound production, a singing quality of tone, and a more in-depth understanding of the playing mechanism involving more than the hands and arms are just some of the enduring principles that permeate our pedagogy today. While there were a considerable number of teachers at these two conservatories who made an impact on countless students, this narrative focuses on two individuals whose innovative approaches set them apart within the broader pedagogical landscape.

Born in Poland, Theodor Leschetizky (1830–1915) eventually moved to Russia, where he pursued a highly successful teaching career at St. Petersburg Conservatory. While he never wrote anything definitive about his teaching, there are many written accounts by his students. Amid the sea of published treatises and methods, the most cutting-edge aspect of Leschetizky's teaching was that he advocated for not having a method. He believed that every student's challenges needed to be approached in different ways. This was corroborated by the way his students depicted his teaching: They all described his pedagogical style differently.

In order to determine the most effective solution for each student, Leschetizky endlessly experimented with different strategies, which led to his keen sensitivity to sound and the precise physical differences needed to create a variety of tonal colors. He placed continual emphasis on touch and tone in his teaching, cultivating a level of sound projection well suited to the demands of larger concert halls and concerto performances. This evolution paralleled the increasingly expansive repertoire composed during that period.

Heinrich Neuhaus (1888–1964) is another significant figure whose name is synonymous with the Russian piano school. His career flourished at the Moscow Conservatory. Through his authoritative book *The Art of Piano Playing* (1973), many generations can still learn from his artistic approach. The main feature of his pedagogical teaching is that artistry must come first—technical execution must always be in service of the musical intentions. This way of thinking was new, as so many teachers and students still adhered to the technical exercises of the past. He felt that the best technical solution would reveal itself once the artistic intention was clear.

English School

As the twentieth century neared, the piano community began to recognize that finger independence and strength, while important, are insufficient for successful performance. Likewise, wrist flexibility alone cannot account for the complexities of the entire playing mechanism. Increasingly, it became evident that traditional technical approaches place undue physical strain on pianists. In an effort to make practice more effective, some educators began exploring how scientific principles could be applied to piano technique.

The most productive of these attempts is the work accomplished by Tobias Matthay (1858–1945). He focused on how finger, hand, and arm movement all relate to one another and relate the speed of key descent to the volume level of sound. Matthay published several books and treatises outlining his method, including *The Act of Touch in All Its Diversity: An Analysis and Synthesis of Pianoforte Tone Production* (1903), *The Fore-Arm Rotation Principle in Pianoforte Playing* (1912), and *The Visible and Invisible in Pianoforte Technique* (1932). In his writings, he explains his thought process regarding relaxation, rotation, and arm weight. While Matthay was drawn to a more systematic approach to explaining piano technique, he did not ignore artistic considerations, such as considering the conceptual flow of music and the timing of rubato.

French School

Restraint, refinement, grace. These are all adjectives associated with what is traditionally considered French playing and are all beautifully illustrated in French repertoire. The defining figures from this school, including Alfred Cortot (1877–1962), Isidor Philipp (1863–1953), and Marguerite Long (1874–1966), emphasized finger independence, a light touch, and subtle wrist movement. They all wrote books with exercises to develop the precise and delicate finger work they wanted their students to achieve.

Developments in the United States

Until this point, much piano instruction was intended for individuals who wanted to be professional musicians. Those in the upper classes of society were usually the only ones who could afford lessons for recreational purposes. Also, the evolution of piano performance and piano pedagogy was limited to European countries. Pianists in the New World, particularly the United States, sought teachers in Europe, learned their methods, and brought their newfound knowledge back home. While the American approach to piano playing remained rooted in European traditions, their innovative use of publications marked a significant shift in pedagogical methods in the United States. With the materials written in Europe, it was the responsibility of the teacher, not the method, to teach students notation and other elements of musical literacy. However, over time, a more sequenced approach for teaching musical notation appeared in American-authored method books.

In 1853, Nathan Richardson, an American who studied in Europe, published the *Modern School for Piano Forte*. He then published the *New Method for the Piano Forte* in 1859 for beginner students. In this latter book, he intersperses "Amusements," accessible dance-like tunes, among the teaching principles and exercises. This feature made the method very popular, as amateurs loved that they could play these short pieces. The piano had come to be regarded as a symbol of social status, accompanied by a growing enthusiasm for piano playing as a leisurely pursuit.

In 1861, Septimus Winner published *The Perfect Guide for the Piano in Which the Instructions Are So Clearly and Simply Treated, as to Make It Unnecessary to Require a Teacher*. Looking at this title from the vantage point of 2026, it seems like this method was the direct precursor to some of the piano apps, YouTube tutorials, and artificial intelligence (AI) tools we see today! It also indicates the overall direction American method books were taking: Successful methods need to present fundamentals in a palatable way, the music needs to be attractive, and the overall mission is "to teach and to please."[2]

The first half of the twentieth century saw progressive teachers in the United States giving more thought to a child's cognitive ability, attention span, and psychomotor development. As pianos became more accessible during this time and were not exclusively reserved for the upper classes, the role of the piano in society was changing. The ability to play the piano became a desired hobby. Many teachers let go of the finger drills so prevalent in years past and experimented with eurhythmics; rote playing; creative activities; and the teaching philosophies of Dalcroze, Orff, and Kodály. Beginning pieces were often well-known tunes arranged for five-finger patterns and using the middle-C hand position.[3]

Reading Approaches

Moving into the middle of the century, as teachers continued to rely more on piano methods, authors provided more sequenced approaches to learning note and rhythm reading. Many methods, such as *John Thompson's Modern Course for the Piano* (1937) by John Thompson (1889–1963), focus on the middle-C approach, where all early melodies that beginners play are confined to the notes a fifth below and a fifth above C. This approach allows students to achieve quick results and play tunes in a relatively short period of time. However, students are limited to playing in that particular position and limited in their understanding of keyboard topography. They play in keys with limited or no accidentals, and if plentiful finger numbers are included, students are often tempted to read by finger number rather than the placement of the note on the staff.[4]

Robert Pace (1924–2010) introduced the multikey method in *Music for Piano* (1961), where students are introduced to playing in many different keys early in their studies. Familiarity with various five-finger patterns is achieved, and beginner students are not restricted to playing on only the white keys. However, there is the risk that students will rely on patterns too much, and they sometimes find it difficult to move to other patterns and different hand shapes.[5]

In her method *The Music Tree* (1955), Frances Clark (1905–1998) advocates for the intervallic method, which encourages students to read notation by intervals and direction. Certain landmark notes are taught as reference points, and students start to read from those landmarks with small intervals, like seconds and thirds, and then gradually move to larger intervals. This enforces a more secure knowledge of notation, but some students do not find the unfamiliar tunes motivating. Furthermore, because beginning pieces only move by seconds and thirds, they do not sound as interesting to students and parents.[6]

These three reading approaches continue to influence method books written in the modern day. Many publications seek the best of all worlds and incorporate all three reading systems into what is now called an eclectic approach.

Professional Development

In the early twentieth century, most piano instructors in the United States were women teaching part time from home. With the ongoing expansion of piano education, a notable shift toward enhanced professional development began to take shape. Journals like *The Étude* (1883–1957) and *The Musician* (1896–1948) gave teachers a peek into the latest teaching trends. The Music Teachers National Association (MTNA) was established in 1876 to connect teachers across the country, offer professional development resources, and eventually help establish nationally accepted standards. Piano pedagogy degrees at both the undergraduate and graduate levels started to be offered at universities, which combined conservatory-style performance training with a formal academic approach to enhance educational knowledge. New journals geared toward the teaching profession, such as *American Music Teacher*, *Piano Quarterly*, *Clavier*, and *Keyboard Companion*, came on the market. Conferences like the MTNA National Conference and the National Conference on Keyboard Pedagogy became a regular part of the professional independent teacher's annual schedule.[7]

Student Events and Assessment

The progress of student development has typically been measured by three types of activities: the traditional recital format, competitions, and assessments. Scattered throughout the school year, these are events that students can work toward and provide external motivation for consistent practice. It is common for teachers of one-to-one piano lessons to have a studio recital at the end of each semester or at the end of the school year. These performances give students the opportunity to work toward a performance goal and share their hard work with families, friends, and others in their studio.

Competitions have also proven to be effective motivators for students. These events are often organized by professional teacher organizations, like MTNA, and can occur at the local, state, and national levels. Other music organizations, such as orchestras, the Chopin Foundation, and the famous piano manufacturer Steinway & Sons, plan similar events.

Finally, graded assessments are another possibility for students to gain feedback from other professionals. Within MTNA, individual state associations may choose to organize their own noncompetitive assessments. For example, the Florida State Music Teachers Association offers Student Day, which are uniform, noncompetitive evaluations in aural skills, written theory, performance skills, and repertoire. A systematic curriculum of twelve levels guides teachers and students through a variety of skills and repertoire with increasing difficulty. Based on their performance, students are awarded a grade or mark.[8] The requirements for these types of assessments vary from state to state.

Similar evaluations with a nationwide standard are offered by the American College of Musicians, commonly known as the Guild Auditions.[9] Based in Toronto, Ontario, the Royal Conservatory of Music runs a large operation that offers piano exams in both Canada and the United States. Under their Certificate Program, they offer a curriculum of ten levels plus the chance to earn an associate or licentiate diploma.[10]

Based on this extensive history that spans three centuries, it is clear that piano teaching benefits from a rich tradition of cultural influence, knowledge passed down through the generations; thoughtful artistic exploration; entrepreneurial approaches; and, most importantly, pedagogues who prioritize their students' musical growth. In many ways, the face of piano teaching has harbored the same characteristics it did three hundred years ago. However, it has also changed drastically as keyboard instruments evolved, teachers experimented with new approaches, and society has transformed.

From Technique to Technology

As piano pedagogy has evolved, so, too, has the technology around us. The increasingly prevalent presence of digital devices, apps, and online platforms has rapidly changed the way we have lived, and it is transforming education, as well. Today's students, particularly those from Generations Z and Alpha, bring with them new perspectives, interests, and ways of engaging with the world. This includes their relationship with technology and how it fits into their daily lives. Just as our approach to technique and overall music learning has grown more responsive to the needs of each student, so, too, must our approach to technology. This evolution reflects a broader truth: To remain effective educators, we must be willing to adapt. Let us now explore how innovations, from film reels to artificial intelligence, have influenced and continue to transform the landscape of piano education.

The twentieth and twenty-first centuries saw enormous amounts of technological growth. From the airplane to film to the internet, society has experienced innovations at such a rapid pace that as one gets used to a product, an improved version has already hit the market. Many inventions have certainly benefited education, and the future holds even more promise as we look ahead to what lies just beyond the horizon. Technology has already made a notable impact on piano teaching and is an important part of our conversation on connecting with Generations Z and Alpha.

Before we discuss the future, let us take a brief journey back in time to the ideas that moved piano pedagogy forward. Sarah Howard and Adrian Mozejko, in their 2015 book chapter about the history of technology in education, classify the movements of technology into three "ages": predigital, personal computer, and internet.[11] This chapter identifies these categories similarly—predigital, digital/person computer, internet—and a fourth type: artificial intelligence.

Predigital Age (1890s–1980s)

Film

The earliest use of film to assist education is believed to have taken place in the 1890s, with more established films produced and used in the 1910s. Instructional videos grew in popularity, and while we do not have many remaining artifacts, we do know that videos were used in piano pedagogy to some extent. In a 1941 article titled "Vitalizing the Music Lesson Through the Visual Sense," Carleton Bullis discusses the use of films in music education.[12] MTNA even formed a subcommittee at this time called the Visual Aids Committee, which aimed to fully realize the benefits that modern visual tools could hold for music education. In 1957, *American Music Teacher* offered a free film for music educators to show their students how pianos were made.[13]

Printing

Printing in the early 1900s was improving and becoming more accessible, and such publishing companies as Schirmer grew and improved.[14] John Schaum and John Thompson published method books with illustrations that became well loved by piano teachers and students across the United States. Eventually, other companies, such as Alfred Publishing Company and Hal Leonard, were founded, and teachers were spoiled with multiple options for piano method books.[15]

Radio and Recorded Sound

Radio marked a groundbreaking advancement in communication, enabling audio broadcasts to reach audiences thousands of miles away. This innovation became possible thanks to the work of Reginald Fessenden, a former employee of Thomas Edison who collaborated with General Electric to develop powerful alternators capable of transmitting voice and sound over long distances.[16] In 1937, the Oklahoma Music Teachers Association included an educational music radio program in its plans for the year.[17] In 1940, MTNA was proud to report that it also had a regular radio broadcast in which top students performed for a widespread audience and had many plans for more educational radio programs across the country.[18]

Radio continued to be used for educational purposes until at least the 1990s. A 1994 issue of *American Music Teacher* shows that there was a radio show for children that often highlighted musical topics, such as how to compose, talent show features, and education about other musical genres.[19] Backing tracks for students were once distributed on record albums, followed by eight-track tapes in the 1960s and 1970s, and then cassette tapes, reflecting the evolution of audio technology in educational and recreational music use.[20]

Television

Televised lessons were used as early as 1956 and offered numerous benefits for students, and many early initiatives in this area were met with enthusiastic and positive responses.[21] Satellite teaching was used to reach more remote places, such as Alaska.[22] Education via television was praised, as it was said to be the "closest thing to real experiences."[23] Eventually, VHS tapes became available, and both teachers and students were able to benefit from instructional piano tapes about topics ranging from repertoire selection to healthy technique.[24]

Electronic Instruments

Ever since the first electronic keyboard protypes in the 1920s (see figure 1.3), the world of nonacoustic pianos has grown and given teachers many wonderful tools with which to work.[25] Improvements to and innovations in electronic instruments included the Baldwin organ, piano labs with electronic pianos, headphones and communication options, and the ability to listen to tapes connected to students' keyboards.[26] The Moog and ARP synthesizers revolutionized sound production by allowing users to generate a wide range of tones from a single keyboard. Although each sound required manual programming, the creative possibilities were groundbreaking. For music educators, these instruments unfolded exciting new avenues for exploration and engagement with piano students.[27]

Figure 1.3 Clavier à Lampe (automatic electrical musical instrument). *Illustration by the author, based on an image in Eugène-H. Weiss,* Phonographes et Musique Mécanique, Bibliothèque des Merveilles *(Paris: Librairie Hachette, June 1930), 16.*

Digital/Personal Computer Age (1970s–Present)

During the 1970s and 1980s, Apple and IBM recognized the potential of integrating personal computers into education. As part of early pilot programs, they provided computers to schools to test the impact of this technology in the classroom. The initiative proved successful, leading to a growing trend for schools investing in computers for student use.[28] As more families, schools, and libraries invested in personal computers, educational games on floppy disks and CD-ROMs attracted parents, educators, and students alike (see figure 1.4).[29] *American Music Teacher* even had a column titled Computer Connection for many years (see figure 1.5). In this column, teachers reviewed various music educational programs available for personal computers.[30] These music education games drilled students on note reading, rhythm, compositional techniques, instruments, music theory, world music, and music history.[31] An article in the *American Music Teacher* states that at the time, these programs were beneficial for supplementing at-home student practice: "Students practice theory drills, rhythm exercises and even solfège regularly during the week with their home computer, receiving accurate, continual feedback as from a tutor."[32]

Figure 1.4 Gameplay from the CD-ROM *Jumpstart Music* (1998), showing the Rhythm Game. *Illustration by the author.*

Computer Connection

Early Childhood Skills

The following descriptions and evaluations are presented as a service to our readers. The inclusion of titles in this department should not be considered an endorsement by MTNA or AMT.

KIDS — Keyboard Introductory Development Series, by Brenna Bailey. Electronic Courseware Systems. © 1989; $100 (four programs).
This program supports the following hardware options:
- Apple II+/IIe, IIc and IIGS
- Yamaha C-1
- Color monitor
- IBM and compatibles
- 256K memory required
- CGA and higher monitors
- 5 1/4" and 3 1/2" disk drives
- Network

Sound sources used:
- MIDI In & MIDI Out (disk 4 only)
- IBM MusicFeature card
- MPU 401 (Roland) compatible
- MIDI Out — Passport (internal)

This program has polyphonic capability. It may be used with earphones for silent operation or with an external speaker for group presentations. *KIDS* is targeted at beginning keyboard students of reading age or younger with parent partner.

Program Description
Each of the four disks contains a single topic program. The first disk is the Zoo Puppet Theater that uses animals to introduce finger number recognition for keyboard playing. Race Car Keys on disk two introduces the identification of the white keys C to G on the keyboard. Dinosaur's Lunch introduces treble staff notation, and Follow Me plays a series of notes that the student must play back on the MIDI keyboard.

Figure 1.5 AMT's Computer Connection column. *Reprinted from* American Music Teacher *41, no. 6 (June/July 1992), with permission of Music Teachers National Association.*

Internet Age (1990s–present)

The internet, which was made public in 1993, revolutionized teacher collaboration, creating an unprecedented space for sharing ideas, resources, and discussions like never before.[33] With the introduction of the MP3 format in the early 1990s and the growing ease of downloading digital audio files, students gained more convenient access to musical repertoire, transforming how they listened to, practiced, and engaged with music.[34] Following the MP3 revolution, streaming platforms like Apple Music and Spotify placed the entire musical world at listeners' fingertips—each offering access to more than 100 million tracks spanning every imaginable genre, culture, and era.[35]

YouTube's invention in 2005 was even more revolutionary, allowing teachers around the world to post instructional videos and giving pianists a public space to post their performances, available for unlimited rewatching by those who wanted to study their playing or simply enjoy listening to them.[36] With the internet also came music games, similar to the CD-ROM educational programs of yesteryear.[37] Social media also allowed teachers to create online spaces for their studios and for students to see their achievements celebrated on a more public forum.[38] The birth of smartphones in 2007 and the iPad in 2010 opened a brand-new world of possibilities that were literally at one's fingertips.[39] Smart device applications now could be used in countless ways to supplement the lesson or classroom (see figure 1.6).

Figure 1.6 The internet age. *Illustration by the author.*

Artificial Intelligence Age

Since the public release of ChatGPT by OpenAI on November 30, 2022, artificial intelligence (AI) has become an inseparable part of conversations about modern technology. AI has already been compared to the industrial revolution by many commentators.[40] What began as experimental research in the 1960s has evolved into a powerful force shaping nearly every industry—including education and the arts. For piano students, AI offers exciting (and sometimes scary) new possibilities: from generating personalized practice routines and offering instant feedback on technique, to helping compose original pieces or exploring music theory in interactive ways. With tools that assist in everything from writing lyrics to planning recitals, AI is becoming a creative companion in the learning process—one that can inspire, support, and expand a student's musical journey.

Heads Up! The Future Is Now

We've explored where we've been and examined the most current trends in both teaching methods and technology. The question now is, Where do we go next?

Teaching Trends

The declining interest in music education was already becoming evident around the middle of the twentieth century. In their two-part article, Sturm, James, Jackson, and Burns, said "The average citizen moved from active participation to a passive culture of music appreciation."[41] In other words, more people were listening to music rather than playing it themselves. The development of recording technology helped to push society in this direction. In some cases, educators tried to highlight the academic benefits of music study, including improved math scores; support for language and literacy; and strengthening executive-functioning skills like focus, memory, and self-regulation.[42] Recently, there has been some opposition to this way of thinking, as there is the belief that music education is simply part of a holistic education—it does not need to be validated or justified by its impact on other subject areas.[43]

Teacher participation in professional associations is on the decline, particularly in the context of ongoing professional learning and development. Activities that once made membership appealing, such as networking, peer support, and sharing advice, are now readily accessible online, especially through social media platforms. Such Facebook groups as the Art of Piano Pedagogy and Piano Teacher Central are considered communities of practice. These groups have become a significant resource for teachers. Participants do not necessarily meet every week or even everyday, but they do value working together while sharing ideas and advice, usually asynchronously.[44]

Prior to the COVID-19 pandemic in 2020, online teaching was pursued by only a few teachers who were willing to experiment with the audio capabilities of the existing video-conferencing platforms. There were also many instructors, students, and parents who did not believe progress could be made in this lesson environment. With the onset of the global pandemic, nearly the entire piano-teaching field was thrust into the online environment, and everyone had to make do—quickly! The well-known phrase "Necessity is the mother of invention" definitely rang true during the COVID years. Teachers quickly came up with ingenious solutions as they worked to replicate the lesson environment for their students as authentically as possible. Instructors learned about new technological tools and discovered how to run their studios with more efficiency and greater offerings. Many workarounds have turned into long-term strategies that are still used today.

The content of typical piano instruction is also changing. While Western classical music is still the foundation of the traditional piano lessons, many teachers are branching out and incorporating popular music in their students' repertoire. The increased awareness of global cultures and the heightened cognizance of equity and inclusion for all have made the piano-teaching field more sensitive to social issues. For example, there is a significant movement toward expanding exposure of repertoire by composers from typically underrepresented groups. The idea of broadening the piano canon has gained attention and traction, offering more choices that are meaningful for each pianist.

In the pursuit of virtuosity in the earlier centuries, the once-highly-valued creative skills of improvisation and composition fell by the wayside. At times, teachers and students were more interested in reaching the highest technical heights possible. However, there has been a sustained resurgence in bringing back these competencies as a part of a holistic piano education.

Technology

At this point in history, we are staring down at the face of AI and wonder about the possibilities it might unlock for us. It is so new that there is excitement, along with anxiety about the unknown and the possible negative effects it might have on humanity. To cope with this new age, let's look at a similar time in history: the beginning of the new millennium. A collection of articles titled "Music Teaching in the New Millennium" offers five tips for approaching new digital trends:

1. **Become familiar with the technology.** Take the time to read user reviews, watch YouTube tutorials, or talk to others who have used it. If the product is popular in music education already, try to attend lectures or conference presentations on the subject and how it is used in piano pedagogy.

2a. **Take time to play with the technology.** Don't be afraid to use the new tool in a recreational manner. If there is a new AI program, just play with it when you have a spare moment. Don't put pressure on yourself to learn it by a deadline if possible.

2b. **Think of how the current technology can benefit your current teaching.** Play stimulates imagination!

3. **Experiment with using these tools in your own teaching!** This takes courage but be confident! You won't know how it'll work with your students until you try!

4. **Assess the results.** What worked? What didn't work? What do you need to change about how you are using this technology in your lessons?

5. **Occasionally revisit the above stages.**[45]

A Thoughtful Approach to Technology

The possibilities that digital tools offer educators are undeniably exciting. However, it's important to approach new technology with intention rather than impulse. Just because a product is new or popular doesn't mean it's the right fit for your studio. Use technology only when it genuinely enhances your students' learning experience.

While a studio filled with the latest gadgets may look impressive, what truly leaves a lasting impact is a teacher who connects meaningfully with their students and uses tools—digital or otherwise—with purpose and clarity. Ultimately, it's not about having the flashiest setup but about fostering the most effective and inspiring learning environment.

Despite the astonishing technological advancements of the past 150 years, one thing remains unchanged: the irreplaceable value of human connection. At the heart of every meaningful learning experience is the relationship between teacher and student. No matter how advanced artificial intelligence becomes, it can never replicate the empathy, intuition, and personal insight that a real teacher brings to the studio. And that teacher is you!

Notes

1 Connie Arrau Sturm, Michael James, Anita Jackson, and Debra Brubaker Burns, "Celebrating 100 Years of Progress in American Piano Teaching: Part I: 1900–1950," *American Music Teacher* 50, no. 2 (October/November 2000): 29–32, http://www.jstor.org/stable/43545086.
2 Marienne Uszler, Stewart Gordon, and Scott McBride Smith, *The Well-Tempered Keyboard Teacher*, 2nd ed. (Schirmer Books, 2000), 352.
3 Sturm, et al., "Celebrating 100 Years, Part I."
4 Jeanine Jacobson, *Professional Piano Teaching: A Comprehensive Piano Pedagogy Textbook for Teaching Elementary-Level Students* (Alfred, 2006), 41–42.
5 Ibid., 42–43.
6 Ibid., 43–44.
7 Connie Arrau Sturm, Michael James, Anita Jackson, and Debra Brubaker Burns, "Celebrating 100 Years of Progress in American Piano Teaching: Part II: 1950–2000," *American Music Teacher* 50, no. 3 (December 2000/January 2001): 24–28, http://www.jstor.org/stable/43545435.
8 "FSMTA Non-Competitive Events," Florida State Music Teachers Association, accessed May 30, 2025, https://www.fmta.org/fsmta-non-competitive-events.html.
9 "Guild Audition," American College of Musicians, accessed June 12, 2025, https://acmglobal.org/guild-audition.
10 "Program Overview: The Royal Conservatory Certificate Program," Royal Conservatory of Music, accessed May 30, 2025, https://www.rcmusic.com/learning/about-the-royal-conservatory-certificate-program/program-overview.
11 Sarah K. Howard and Adrian Mozejko, "Considering the History of Digital Technologies in Education," in *Teaching and Digital Technologies: Big Issues and Critical Questions*, ed. Michael Henderson and Geoff Romeo, 157–68 (Cambridge University Press, 2015), https://doi.org/10.1017/CBO9781316091968.017.

12 Carleton Bullis, "Vitalizing the Music Lesson Through the Visual Sense," *Bulletin of the Music Teachers National Association* 6, no. 2 (November 1941): 16–19, http://www.jstor.org/stable/43528481.

13 Front matter, *American Music Teacher* 6, no. 5 (May/June 1957), http://www.jstor.org/stable/43536083.

14 "Schirmer's Library of Music Classics," Willis Piano Music, accessed June 12, 2025, https://www.willispianomusic.com/search/search.action?_c&seriesfeature=SCHLIB&menuid=14537&subsiteid=264&&sorttype=popularcategory&page=1&resultsperpage=30.

15 "Our History," Alfred Music, accessed May 16, 2025, https://www.alfred.com/history/; Heather Sowers, "The Success Story That Is Hal Leonard," *Winona Daily News*, January 16, 2015, https://winonadailynews.com/special-section/pieces-of-the-past/article_eef2080b-3743-53da-ad5a-a9bcea4e5a42.html.

16 "1890s–1930s: Radio," Imagining the Internet: A History and Forecast, Elon University accessed May 16, 2025, https://www.elon.edu/u/imagining/time-capsule/150-years/back-1890-1930/.

17 "Oklahoma State Music Teachers' Association," *Advisory Council Bulletin (Music Teachers' National Association)* 2, no. 1 (December 1937): 6, http://www.jstor.org/stable/43526209.

18 Edith Lucille Robbins, "Inspiring Reports from State and Local Music Associations," *Bulletin of the Music Teachers National Association* 5, no. 2 (October 1940): 16–45, http://www.jstor.org/stable/43527011.

19 "Impromptu," *American Music Teacher* 44, no. 1 (August/September 1994): 4–10, http://www.jstor.org/stable/43542719.

20 "History of the 8-Track Tapes," RecordingHistory.org, accessed May 17, 2025, https://recording-history.org/history-of-8-track-tapes/.

21 E. L. Lancaster, "Audio-Visual Programming for the Piano Class," *Clavier* 16 (1976): 29–32; "West Central Division," *American Music Teacher* 5, no. 3 (January/February 1956): 10–28, http://www.jstor.org/stable/43536040.

22 Charnel Anderson, *New Media for Instruction 1: Technology in American Education, 1650–1900* (Office of Education, US Department of Health, Education, and Welfare, 1962), https://research.ebsco.com/linkprocessor/plink?id=9c70ce66-8668-3061-8d63-88a2e42e3e3c.

23 William King, cited in Neil Selwyn, *Education and Technology: Key Issues and Debates* (Continuum International, 2011), 54.

24 "Industry News," *American Music Teacher* 38, no. 1 (September/October 1988): 8, http://www.jstor.org/stable/43542123.

25 Eugène-H. Weiss, *Phonographes et Musique Mécanique*, Bibliothèque des Merveilles (Librairie Hachette, June 1930), 16.

26 Front matter, *American Music Teacher* 8, no. 3 (January/February 1959), http://www.jstor.org/stable/43532081; Front matter, *American Music Teacher* 19, no. 2 (November/December 1969), http://www.jstor.org/stable/43537433; Front matter,

American Music Teacher 19, no. 4 (February/March 1970), http://www.jstor.org/stable/43533611.

27 K. D. Renfrow, "The Development and Evaluation of Objectives for Educating Graduate Piano Pedagogy Students to Use Computer and Keyboard Technology" (PhD diss., University of Oklahoma, 1991), ProQuest (9135052).

28 Howard and Mozejko, "Considering the History."

29 "JumpStart Music," JumpStart Wiki, Fandom, accessed May 17, 2025, https://jstart.fandom.com/wiki/JumpStart_Music.

30 Christine D. Hermanson and Carolyn Inabinet, Computer Connection, *American Music Teacher* 41, no. 6 (June/July 1992): 10–11, http://www.jstor.org/stable/43547394.

31 Brent A. Andrews, "New Computer Software, CD-ROMs, and Videodiscs in K–12 Music Education: What Music Educators and Media Specialists Need to Know: A Selected Annotated Bibliography" (graduate research paper 1712, University of Northern Iowa, 1996).

32 Barbara English Maris, Gary L. Ingle, Joan Reist, et al., "Music Teaching in the New Millennium," *American Music Teacher* 49, no. 6 (June/July 2000): 21–53, http://www.jstor.org/stable/43549056.

33 "World Wide Web Timeline," Pew Research Center, March 11, 2014, https://www.pewresearch.org/internet/2014/03/11/world-wide-web-timeline/.

34 "MP3," Make Software: Change the World, Computer History Museum, accessed May 17, 2025, https://www.computerhistory.org/makesoftware/exhibit/mp3/.

35 Naveen Kumar, "Apple Music Users Statistics 2025 (Revenue and Market Share)," Demand Sage, August 25, 2025, https://www.demandsage.com/apple-music-statistics/.

36 James Hardy, "Who Invented YouTube: The Visionaries Behind the Digital Revolution," History Cooperative, December 5, 2023, https://historycooperative.org/who-invented-youtube/.

37 "Music Games," CrazyGames, accessed May 17, 2025, https://www.crazygames.com/t/music.

38 Melody Morrison, "Gen Z and Gen Alpha: Who Are They and How Do We Teach Them?" *Florida Music Director* 77, no. 2 (2023): 26–31.

39 History.com Editors, "Steve Jobs Debuts the iPhone," History, updated May 27, 2025, https://www.history.com/this-day-in-history/january-9/steve-jobs-debuts-the-iphone; "iPad Tablet Computer with Adapter," National Museum of American History Behring Center, Smithsonian Institution, accessed June 12, 2025, https://americanhistory.si.edu/collections/nmah_1456024.

40 Janna Anderson and Lee Rainie, "Artificial Intelligence and the Future of Humans," Pew Research Center, December 10, 2018, https://www.pewresearch.org/internet/2018/12/10/artificial-intelligence-and-the-future-of-humans/.

41 Sturm et al., "Celebrating 100 Years: Part II."

42. E. L. Lancaster, "Music Students and Academic Achievement: Two New Looks," *American Music Teacher* 71, no. 2 (October/November 2021): 10–12. https://www.jstor.org/stable/27143354; Royal Conservatory of Music, *The Benefits of Music Education* (Royal Conservatory of Music, April 2014), https://rcmusic-kentico-cdn.s3.amazonaws.com/rcm/media/main/learning/rcm_benefitsofmusiceducation_whitepaper.pdf.
43. Aaron Allen, "STEM vs. STEAM: Advocating for the Return of Art and Music in School Curriculums," National Newspaper Publishers Association, accessed June 19, 2025, https://nnpa.org/stem-vs-steam-advocating-for-the-return-of-art-and-music-in-school-curriculums/; American Academy of Arts and Sciences, *Art for Life's Sake: The Case for Arts Education* (American Academy of Arts and Sciences, 2021).
44. Christiana Shelenberger Roe, "Pedagogical Trends of Note-Reading in Piano Teachers' Facebook Groups," *MTNA e-Journal* (September 2021), https://www.mtna.org/MTNA/Stay_Informed/MTNA_e-Journal/MTNA_e-Journal_Archives/September_2021.aspx.
45. Maris et al., "Music Teaching."

2 What's in a Generation?

What is a generation? What do we mean when we talk about generational research? A dictionary will describe a generation as those born and living at the same time, but in this book, we refer to what are called "social generations." As one study puts it, a social generation consists of "people within a delineated population who experience the same significant events within a given period of time."[1] So this definition does not encompass everyone who is alive at the same time but rather those groups who are bonded together because they experienced similar social constructs and events in their upbringing.[2] The Library of Congress states, "For the most part, date ranges for generations are based around common economic, social, or political factors that happened during formative years."[3] Based on these definitions and existing literature, the average date range for a generation is about fifteen to twenty years.[4]

The book *Gen Z in Work* brings up a six-point framework to better define each generation:

1 A formative or traumatic event
2 Significant demographic changes
3 Periods linked to the group's collective success or failure
4 The establishment of a "sacred space" that preserves collective memory
5 Influential mentors or heroes, contrasted by antiheroes
6 A community of individuals who share support and knowledge[5]

The generation that one is born into certainly seems to have an impact on the individuals of that time. In fact, a generational psychologist states, "The era when you were born has a substantial influence on your behaviors, attitudes, values, and personality traits. In fact, when you were born has a larger effect on your personality and attitudes than the family who raised you does."[6] While this statement may seem bold, it underscores the profound impact that generational context can have on shaping an individual's development and worldview.

Some may be wondering, "Do these social generations strictly refer to those in the United States, or do these characteristics apply to other parts of the world, as well?" While the practice of naming and analyzing generations is primarily rooted in Western culture, and while some countries may retain other titles and slightly different groupings, these generational labels can still be applied broadly to individuals around the world who were born during the same time periods.[7] However, the discussion of this book is based on the history and culture of the United States, especially when summarizing generations of pre-internet days. As global connectivity has increased through the internet, it has become more common to group generations across countries for such purposes as education and marketing, reflecting shared experiences shaped by worldwide access to information, media, and technology. For example, while Generation Z and its associated cultural and social trends are heavily influenced by American culture, the term *Generation Z* refers to individuals born between the mid-1990s and the early 2010s worldwide. This generation exists across numerous countries and cultures, with some characteristics and behaviors shaped by local contexts and experiences.

Generational Differences

Why Generations Are Important

Have you ever heard an older adult say something along the lines of, "Kids these days just don't understand," or "We were the last generation to experience x and y"? Our human nature tends to gravitate toward staying within our established comfort zones and familiar experiences. If someone else is different, then it can be easy to judge that behavior as incorrect. In fact, each generation tends to view the next generation as flawed and self-centered. This has been the reality for not decades but centuries and millenniums. In ancient Greece, children were said to have bad manners, and in the Middle Ages, guild masters complained that they had poor apprentices. In these cases, the issue at hand was likely that the younger groups were merely unexperienced and ignorant. And yet, as a wise professor at the University of California Department of Medicine writes, "Each aging cohort looks upon the youth and believes they have identified a fundamental change in the species."[8] In 2013, *Time* magazine published a cover story titled "The Me Me Me Generation," echoing an accusation that many older adults already held toward millennials—that today's young people are entitled and self-absorbed.[9] However, some were surprised and humbled to learn that this wasn't a new critique. In 1976, *New York* magazine ran a cover story declaring the 1970s as "The 'Me' Decade," mocking the perceived narcissism of the then-young Baby Boomer generation.[10]

It's often difficult (at least at first) to understand another group of people, especially if we don't comprehend why or what they are doing. This is one of the reasons generational research is beneficial. It helps both the newer and more seasoned generations to look outside their box and view life from the perspective of the other. Additionally, it is important to shed light on the fact that generations influence each other and build on the actions and views of those who came before. As teachers, it is especially crucial to study and understand the upbringing and society shaping our students today.

Although examining generational traits can be highly insightful, it's important to remember that these are broad generalizations. Our research can highlight recurring patterns, but these should be viewed as overarching themes rather than definitive rules. There will always be outliers and people who may have experienced a unique upbringing in an uncommon household or geographic area. And of course, because no two students are the same, a teacher should never abandon the habit of getting to know each student on an individual basis. Stereotyping every student who belongs to a certain generation will never be the practice of a good educator. These observations and summaries of age groups should only serve to assist in adapting teaching and communication methods to more effectively reach the generations who take lessons in our studios.

Generations provide the opportunity to look at people both by their place in the life cycle—whether a young adult, a middle-aged parent, or a retiree—and by their membership in a cohort of individuals born at a similar time.[11] Mark McCrindle, the social researcher who coined the term *Generation Alpha*, states that generational research is now a "mainstream field" in sociology and the academic world. He further asserts that there are more generations mixed in the household and workplace than ever before and that we must put forth effort to understand generational nuances. McCrindle goes on to write that it is also important for human resources, marketing, and leadership of businesses and organizations to understand the different generations, as the employees and the companies' customer bases represent various age groups. He even stresses that companies who do not make an effort to engage and communicate with newer generations will eventually disappear due to irrelevance.[12]

Overview of Generations

The GI Generation: The Greatest Generation (1901–1924)

The GI Generation—named for their significant role in World War II—is also known as the Greatest Generation, a term popularized in recent decades by newscaster Tom Brokaw.[13] The high praise that Brokaw and others give this group is certainly not without reason. Members of the Greatest Generation are known for their resilience and self-reliance, often pulling themselves up by their bootstraps and doing whatever it takes to make ends meet.

This generation witnessed much in their early years. During the roaring twenties, women received the right to vote, society focused on keeping children out of factories, many Americans moved to the city, and flappers symbolized "economic, political, and sexual freedom for women."[14] Many of the GI Generation were children during the Great Depression, which resulted in innovation and creativity during their upbringing. Recreation was not on the list of priorities for struggling families, so the children of this era came up with their own games and toys. Sadly, some of these children also endured abuse due to stressed-out parents facing extreme financial and emotional hardship.

Then, ten years after the stock market crashed, a world war began and was the definition of an "all hands on deck" situation. While 16.4 million men were off fighting in combat, 1 in 4 women filled in a job that would have otherwise been held by a man while the troops were away.[15] Women also worked in many other roles, including airplane technicians, radio operators, pilots, and nurses. The iconic Rosie the Riveter became the face of women in World War II and kept spirits up for those at home and abroad.[16] After World War II, the nation experienced economic prosperity and peace, and many Americans moved to the suburbs, bought a house, and lived the American dream.

Education

Members of the GI Generation could land a decent job with only a high school education. After World War II, many veterans took advantage of the newly passed GI Bill and received a college education, furthering their chances of securing a well-paying position. Many members of this generation possessed street smarts that also served them well, as they showed an "ability to know how to survive and make do and solve problems."[17]

Characteristics

Members of the Greatest Generation are known to be frugal consumers, likely due to growing up during the Depression and surviving during the days of World War II. This group is also said to be driven, patriotic, and team oriented, stemming from their deep dedication to their country during global conflict.[18] The Greatest Generation holds a high sense of civic duty and social responsibility, and their aspirations are often framed in terms of service rather than personal gain or fame. Many members of this generation express desires to contribute to society through careers in teaching, politics, social work, and public service. Despite economic hardship and global conflict, many maintain a forward-looking, purposeful mindset and high levels of resilience and optimism. This generation also worked to cultivate supportive family environments and better lives for their children (see figure 2.1).[19]

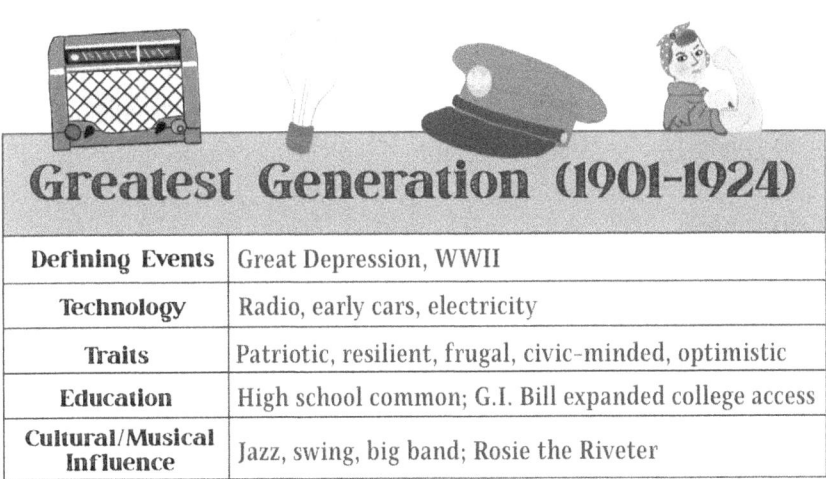

Greatest Generation (1901-1924)

Defining Events	Great Depression, WWII
Technology	Radio, early cars, electricity
Traits	Patriotic, resilient, frugal, civic-minded, optimistic
Education	High school common; G.I. Bill expanded college access
Cultural/Musical Influence	Jazz, swing, big band; Rosie the Riveter

Figure 2.1 Characteristics of the Greatest Generation. *Illustration by the author.*

The Silent Generation (1925–1945)

This generation was known as the Silent Generation since 1951, when *Time* magazine published an article describing this group's tendency to fly under the radar while working hard and following rules and tradition.[20]

Children of the Silent Generation were told they were to be seen but not heard, which likely contributed to their overall conformist demeanor.[21] This era saw the golden age of the radio and the ability to hear live broadcasts and breaking news over this new household device. The television also became a staple that families enjoyed in their residences. As the silents grew, they enjoyed a booming job market and postwar economic prosperity. The 1950s were a time of exciting modernism and a peek at a technology-infused future. As society moved away from agricultural careers and toward knowledge-based jobs that required specific skills, more education and training became necessary.[22]

While people of this era are thought of as those who would never ruffle feathers or garner any attention, the Silent Generation did participate in cultural and political movements that did not always fit this description. As teenagers and young adults, members of the Silent Generation embraced the rise of rock and roll, adopting hip styles in their clothing, speech, and daily habits.[23] Additionally, many leaders of the Civil Rights Movement belonged to the Silent Generation, including Dr. Martin Luther King Jr. and Jesse Jackson.[24] While the Silent Generation is not often associated with the hippie movement, many of the original hippies who achieved some real change in societal issues were silents.[25] Another reason this generation came to be known as the Silent Generation is that for many years none of its members held the office of president of the United States. This changed in 2020, when Joseph Biden (b. 1942) was elected, finally giving the Silent Generation presidential representation.

Education

While it was previously acceptable for a young person to begin their occupational journey at twelve years old, for the Silent Generation, it was expected that one would finish high school. In fact, 86 percent of silents are reported to have at least a high school education—a much higher percentage than those who came before them. It also was more common for one to attend a four-year university before entering the job market, with one-third of silents attaining a college degree.[26]

Characteristics

Members of the Silent Generation are known to have accepted differences and to have believed in equality.[27] This demographic has shown themselves to be open to progressive change through their part in countercultural movements. Compared to other generations, the silents tend to be less cynical and more likely to trust others. This may be attributed to the low crime rates and the overall sense of national relief and unity that characterized the 1950s and early 1960s. Overall, the silent generation may be one that is often overlooked, but this demographic is characterized by a solid group of family-oriented hard workers who look for the good in others (see figure 2.2).[28]

Baby Boomers (1946–1964)

After the GI Generation settled down, they were ready to start families, and the timing couldn't have been better! The United States was in a state of sheer optimism, as they had won the war and were enjoying a booming economy. Between 1946 and 1964, 76.4 million babies were born in the United States.[29] Boomers were the first to grow up watching television and the first to experience events in real time, such as man walking on the moon, the Cuban missile crisis, and the assassination of JFK.[30] Baby boomers could

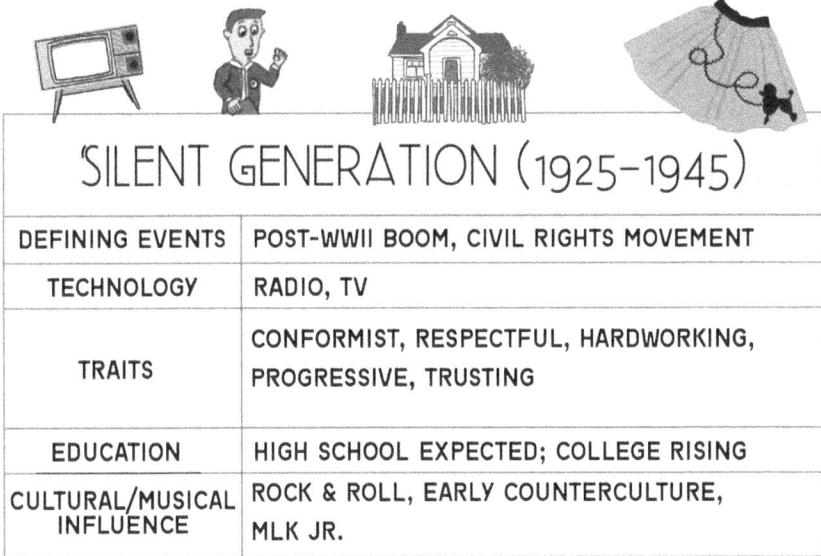

SILENT GENERATION (1925–1945)	
DEFINING EVENTS	POST-WWII BOOM, CIVIL RIGHTS MOVEMENT
TECHNOLOGY	RADIO, TV
TRAITS	CONFORMIST, RESPECTFUL, HARDWORKING, PROGRESSIVE, TRUSTING
EDUCATION	HIGH SCHOOL EXPECTED; COLLEGE RISING
CULTURAL/MUSICAL INFLUENCE	ROCK & ROLL, EARLY COUNTERCULTURE, MLK JR.

Figure 2.2 Characteristics of the Silent Generation. *Illustration by the author.*

be considered quite spoiled when compared to previous generations, as their parents did not want them to go without, and most enjoyed a prosperous childhood due to strong economic stability and a sense of national peace and security.[31] Examples of how boomers differ from previous generations is exemplified in part by the hippie movement that stemmed from individualism and mass protests against the Vietnam War drafts in 1973.[32]

Furthermore, interestingly the word *get* versus *give* increased in the literature of this time. *Give* was more common than *get* until the 1940s, but in the 1970s, when boomers were teenagers, the word *get* surged. Words like *identity* and *unique* were also popular terms at this time and onward.[33]

After their days of student activism, which included fights for women's rights, racial equality, and environmental concerns, boomers settled down at young ages. Because buying a house was attainable, as home prices remained low, boomers often purchased a home, married, and started a family before the age of thirty.[34] Many boomers married young, and divorce was the result of many of these unions, with twice as many boomers divorced in the 2020s, compared to the silent generation in the 1990s.[35]

The health of the economy further benefited boomers in the 1980s and 1990s, as they enjoyed a comfortable, stable economy and built up their wealth and assets. In the workforce, boomers are strong supporters of the corporate environment and enjoyed the structure of a 9-to-5 lifestyle for many years, though some have found satisfaction in a more flexible work life with the rise of remote work in their later years.[36]

Education

Finishing high school was expected for boomers. Of the 90 percent of boomers who finished high school, 17 percent of men and 14 percent of women went on to complete a bachelor's degree.[37] While more boomers attended college than before, in the 1960s and 1970s, it was still possible to land a good job with just a high school degree, as manufacturing jobs were plentiful when boomers first entered the workforce. However, blue-collar jobs declined in the 1980s, when the increase in technology and transfer of industries to overseas left millions of steel and auto workers without work. This greatly widened the divide between those who were prosperous and those who were struggling financially.[38] Laid-off employees in these situations were forced to complete a college degree or find a new career.

Characteristics

Baby boomers have often seemed to be the spotlight of society. Some see them as level-headed, hardworking folks, while others claim that they tend to act in a self-centered manner.[39] The individualism that boomers were known for grew into materialism in the 1980s, as they amassed wealth and assets and were known for heavy purchasing. In recent years, boomers are reported to be gloomy and pessimistic about their quality of life and financial situation, while they ironically have enjoyed the highest income of any living generation for many years and are also more likely than other groups to hold retirement funds, stocks, and bonds.[40] In fact, the baby boomers' combined net worth makes up half of all the wealth in the United States.[41]

Other traits of boomers include a strong work ethic and a loyalty to structure and traditional values.[42] Boomers also say that they generally feel young for their age. Boomers are generally known to be a bit hesitant to adopt technology—two-thirds of boomers say they are anxious that their devices are not working correctly.[43] However, more than half of them use some sort of social media platform (usually Facebook) and have adapted to technology, even though they are not digital natives (see figure 2.3).

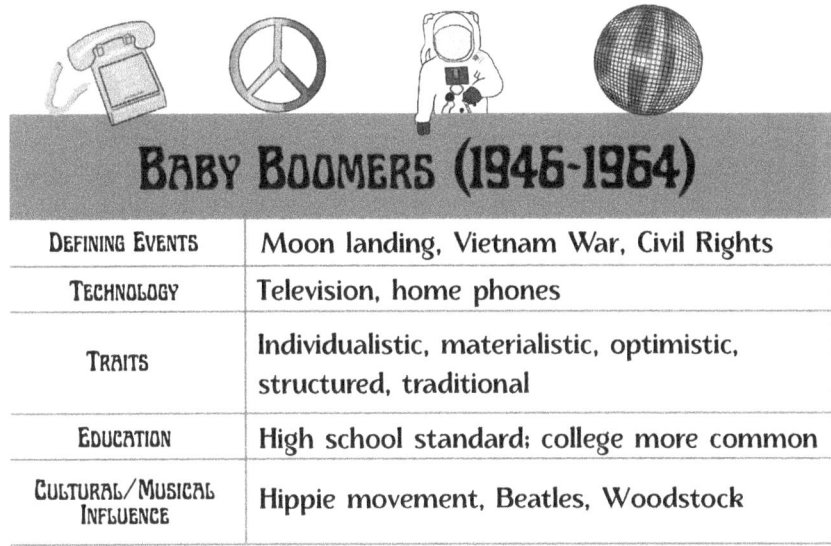

BABY BOOMERS (1946-1964)	
Defining Events	Moon landing, Vietnam War, Civil Rights
Technology	Television, home phones
Traits	Individualistic, materialistic, optimistic, structured, traditional
Education	High school standard; college more common
Cultural/Musical Influence	Hippie movement, Beatles, Woodstock

Figure 2.3 Characteristics of the baby boomers. *Illustration by the author.*

Generation X (1965–1980)

Often referred to as the "middle child" because they come between the domineering generations of boomers and millennials, Gen X experienced technological excitement like never before as well as new challenges. When they were children, Generation X experienced growing distrust in the government and political tension because of such events as Watergate, the decline of the stock market, and Operation Desert Storm.[44] Gen X latchkey kids were often left unattended, as the household of two working parents gradually became more dominant and kids were often told to "come home when the streetlight turns on."

As Gen X grew, they witnessed tragic events, such as the explosion of the *Challenger* on live TV, but they also watched the fall of the Berlin Wall and the end of the Cold War. Generation X was also the first group to attend integrated schools beginning in kindergarten, and the concept of racial integration was further promoted by *Sesame Street*, which exposed them to many other worldviews and races.[45] Although Generation X grew up during a time marked by economic uncertainty, with shifting family dynamics and a growing distrust in institutions, they also experienced a golden era of pop culture. From Saturday-morning cartoons like *He-Man* and *Transformers*, to iconic toys like the Rubik's Cube and Atari consoles and such blockbuster films as *Star Wars* and *E.T.*, their formative years were filled with cultural touchstones. Music from artists like Prince, Madonna, and the Clash provided the soundtrack to their youth—much of which remains beloved and influential today.

Gen X also experienced the rise of personal computers and still is the largest demographic of desktop computer users today. In fact, many members of Gen X were pioneers in the early computer days who held a unique perspective on technology. Gen X used bulky CRT monitors; experienced the first days of dial-up internet, along with early email and chat-room systems; and witnessed the growth of the digital age with appreciation of the past.[46] While all living generations experienced the aftermath of 9/11 and the stock market crash of 2008, the group that was hit hardest was Gen X, as they were young, and many were either fresh in their careers or approaching their peak earning period. Partly due to their skepticism and financial setbacks, Gen X has a track record of marrying later in life but remains largely family focused.

Education

Gen X was extrinsically motivated to get a quality education, and in the 1980s, three out of four Gen Xers stated being well-off was important to them. They also maintained a "reach for the stars" mentality, and many dreamed of becoming lawyers, doctors, and engineers. Although roughly two out of three Gen Xers did not attain their career goals, their ambition resulted in higher levels of education than the boomers had achieved.[47] By this point, high school education was a given for Gen X, and by age 33, 18 percent of men and 20 percent of women had completed a four-year degree.[48]

Characteristics

Often labeled as pessimistic, Generation X is more accurately described as cautious—and with good reason. Growing up, they witnessed a cascade of unsettling events: the Watergate scandal, the *Challenger* explosion, the Cold War's looming threat, and the rise of the AIDS crisis. These formative experiences instilled a healthy skepticism and a sense of vigilance. As adults, many Gen Xers have faced economic recessions, the bursting of the dot-com bubble, and the 2008 financial crisis—often without the safety nets enjoyed by previous generations. Yet despite these challenges, Gen X has proven to be remarkably savvy and self-reliant. They've adapted to rapid technological change, pioneered the gig economy, and continue to roll with the punches with a quiet resilience that defines their character (see figure 2.4).

Generation Y (1981–1995)

Generation Y, often referred to as "millennials," are the most planned and wanted generation in history and have been told that the future is in their hands.[49] Sometimes millennials are called the "echo boom" because in 2019, they became the largest generation, surpassing boomers. As children and teenagers, millennials experienced a moment of national trauma similar to what Generation X felt during the *Challenger* explosion—witnessing the events of 9/11 unfold live on television, along with the fear and uncertainty that gripped the country in its aftermath.[50]

Aside from the tragedy of September 11, the childhoods of millennials were filled with a vibrant mix of toys, games, and early digital adventures. They

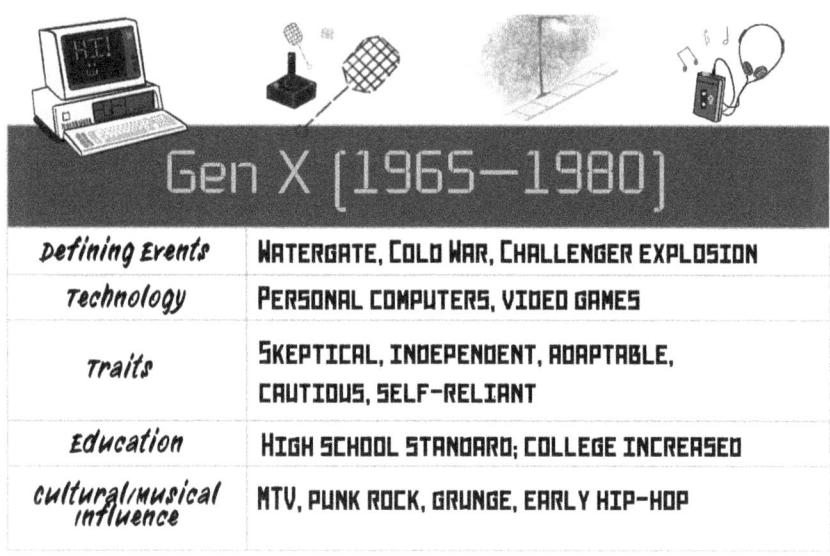

Figure 2.4 Characteristics of Gen X. *Illustration by the author.*

grew up collecting Beanie Babies, trading Pokémon cards, and playing with Tamagotchis. Afternoons were spent on Game Boys, early dial-up internet, or navigating pixelated worlds in the *Oregon Trail* and *Neopets*. Shows like *Blue's Clues*, *Rugrats*, and *Sailor Moon* lit up their screens, while the sound of AOL's "You've got mail" and dial-up internet became a familiar part of their digital awakening. Places like McDonald's and Toys 'R' Us were vibrant hubs of childhood joy, thoughtfully designed and marketed to captivate young imaginations. For many millennials, these spaces hold cherished memories of colorful play areas, catchy jingles, and the excitement of weekend visits.

Now deep into adulthood, many millennials find themselves longing for the carefree days of their youth—moments that feel increasingly distant and irretrievable. This nostalgia is vividly reflected on modern social media, where entire pages are devoted to celebrating the pop culture of the '80s, '90s, and early 2000s. These digital spaces share images of old toys, commercials, and snack brands, often paired with sentimental music, offering fleeting but powerful glimpses back into childhood. For a generation shaped by rapid change, these nostalgic corners of the internet serve as comforting time capsules. A foreshadowing of their financial future would be the recession of 2008, during which many millennials lived with their parents and constantly heard talk of unpredictable markets and rising unemployment. Despite the sleek, optimistic allure of see-through gadgets, Y2K design, and Frutiger Aero aesthetics—which suggested a future full of innovation and limitless potential—millennials came of age under the shadow of financial uncertainty, acutely aware that they were growing up in an era of increasing economic instability.

Generations of the twentieth century would always improve as time went on, but some scholars have remarked that millennials in the West are the first modern generation to be economically worse off than their parents.[51] Millennials have paid the consequences of previous choices in economic structure and suffer rising unemployment rates, school debt, and inflation. As a result, many members of Gen Y became minimalists to save on costs and spread such ideas as tiny homes.

Perhaps the change in society was one to spark innovation in this generation, as millennials are quite creative and entrepreneurial. Every social media platform at the time of this writing was created by a millennial: MySpace, Facebook, Tumblr, Instagram, TikTok, and Snapchat, to name a few. Not surprisingly, Gen Y is the first to live completely online, and many have formed their identities early on based on social media. Millennials are still chronically online and use tools of the digital age for everything, from dating on Bumble or Hinge, to online shopping on Amazon.

Although millennials got a rough start in today's economy, an updated look at how millennials are doing reveals a much more positive outlook than the articles of a few years ago. While it is still much more difficult for a millennial to purchase a house, it has not proven impossible for them, and many have been able to purchase a home with the help of parents or as a result of their own discipline. Millennials are getting a later start on building their assets, not only because of inflation and rising home prices, but also because many have gone to graduate school and are not fully entering the job market until their late twenties or early thirties. Hopefully, millennials will also begin to bring in bigger paychecks as they progress in their careers. This will help with their student loans, which are on average $47,400 for a four-year degree.[52]

One of the defining shifts with the millennial generation is their approach to marriage. This is the first time in American history that the majority of adults aged twenty-five to thirty-nine are unmarried. In parallel, the United States is also experiencing its lowest birth rates on record, marking a significant cultural and demographic departure from previous generations. Many of those who decide to have children have taken up the gentle-parenting movement, which has spread on TikTok and Instagram. This form of parenting is built heavily on empathy and involves setting expectations well in advance so that negative conditioning or outbursts in the moment do not occur.[53] There are mixed opinions on gentle parenting, ranging from extreme support from professionals and parents on social media to unfiltered criticism with proven consequences of this method.[54] The reason a millennial may take up gentle parenting is that they do not want to be like their parents, who may have been either too authoritarian or neglectful.[55] Millennials are a distinct and influential generation, poised to shape the future as they take on leadership roles, raise the next generation, and gradually replace older cohorts as the primary decision makers in society.

Education

When asked what is different about them compared to their parents, millennials often say, "Education." This group is marked by many first-generation college students, with more than one in three possessing a four-year college degree by their late twenties.[56] In addition to the growing demand for specialized degrees in today's job market, many millennials—raised with encouragement and a strong sense of individual worth—have been motivated to pursue higher education. Messages saying that they were special and capable of achieving great things have often been viewed as negative. However, these efforts also helped foster self-confidence and goal setting, driving many young people toward academic and professional success when these traits were coupled with discipline and grit.

Characteristics

Often dubbed the "Me Generation," millennials have grown into a thoughtful, resilient, and socially conscious cohort. Despite facing economic setbacks, rising living costs, and the challenges of entering adulthood during uncertain times, they continue to strive for progress—both personally and globally. This generation values empathy, inclusivity, and innovation, and they remain optimistic about creating a better future. With a strong sense of purpose and a willingness to adapt, millennials are not only raising the next generation but also reshaping the world with open minds and compassionate hearts (see figure 2.5).

MILLENNIALS (1981–1995)	
DEFINING EVENTS	9/11, 2008 Recession, rise of internet
TECHNOLOGY	Internet, smartphones, social media
TRAITS	Empathetic, entrepreneurial, anxious, inclusive, nostalgic
EDUCATION	High college attendance; student debt common
CULTURAL/MUSICAL INFLUENCE	Pop-punk, early EDM, 90s/2000s nostalgia

Figure 2.5 Characteristics of the millennials. *Illustration by the author.*

Notes

1. Jane Pilcher, "Mannheim's Sociology of Generations: An Undervalued Legacy," *British Journal of Sociology* 45, no. 3 (September 1994): 481–95, https://doi.org/10.2307/591659.
2. Ibid.
3. "Generations," Library of Congress: Research Guides, accessed June 12, 2025, https://guides.loc.gov/consumer-research/market-segments/generations.
4. Corey Seemiller and Meghan Grace, *Generation Z: A Century in the Making* (Routledge, 2018), https://doi.org/10.4324/9780429442476.
5. Karina Ochis, *Gen Z in Work: A Practical Guide to Engaging Employees Across the Generations* (Routledge, 2024), https://doi.org/10.4324/9781032722696; David Wyatt, *Out of the Sixties* (Cambridge University Press, 1993).
6. Jean M. Twenge, *Generations: The Real Differences Between Gen Z, Millennials, Gen X, Boomers, and Silents—and What They Mean for America's Future* (Atria Books, 2023).
7. Matt Rosenberg, *Generational Names in the United States: Gen X, Millennials, and Other Generations Through the Years* (ThoughCo., updated June 8, 2019), https://ifmahouston.org/downloads/Meeting_Presentations/names_of_generations_1435472.pdf.
8. Gurpreet Dhaliwal, "The Greatest Generation," *JAMA* 323, no. 17 (May 5, 2020): 1696–97, https://doi.org/10.1001/jama.2020.2972.
9. Joel Stein, "Millennials: The Me Me Me Generation," *Time*, May 20, 2013, https://time.com/247/millennials-the-me-me-me-generation/.

10 Tom Wolfe, "The 'Me' Decade," *New York*, August 23, 1976.
11 Michael Dimock, "Where Millennials End and Generation Z Begins," Pew Research Center, January 17, 2019, https://www.pewresearch.org/short-reads/2019/01/17/where-millennials-end-and-generation-z-begins/.
12 "The Generations Defined," McCrindle, accessed May 30, 2025, https://mccrindle.com.au/article/topic/demographics/the-generations-defined/.
13 J. M. Bullinger, *Reagan's "Boys" and the Children of the Greatest Generation: U.S. World War II Memory, 1984 and Beyond* (Routledge, 2019).
14 History.com Editors, "The Roaring Twenties," History, last updated August 28, 2025, https://www.history.com/articles/roaring-twenties-history; History.com Editors, "Flappers," History, last updated May 28, 2025, https://www.history.com/articles/flappers.
15 "WWII Veteran Statistics: The Legacy of the WWII Generation," National WWII Museum New Orleans, accessed May 2, 2025, https://www.nationalww2museum.org/war/wwii-veteran-statistics.
16 "History at a Glance: Women in World War II," The National WWII Museum New Orleans, accessed May 2, 2025, https://www.nationalww2museum.org/students-teachers/student-resources/research-starters/women-wwii.
17 Kate Zernike, "Generation OMG," *New York Times*, March 8, 2009, https://archive.nytimes.com/www.nytimes.com/learning/teachers/featured_articles/20090313friday.html.
18 Julia Kagan, "The Greatest Generation: Definition and Characteristics," Investopedia, updated April 28, 2025, https://www.investopedia.com/terms/t/the_greatest_generation.asp.
19 Jenni Menon Mariano and George E. Vaillant, "Youth Purpose Among the 'Greatest Generation,'" *Journal of Positive Psychology* 7, no. 4 (2012): 281–93, https://doi.org/10.1080/17439760.2012.686624.
20 Seemiller and Grace, *Generation Z*, 4.
21 Ibid.
22 Thomas D. Snyder, ed., *120 Years of American Education: A Statistical Portrait* (National Center for Education Statistics, US Department of Education, Office of Educational Research and Improvement, January 1993), https://nces.ed.gov/pubs93/93442.pdf.
23 Alicja Zelazko, "Millennial," *Encyclopedia Britannica*, last updated September 13, 2025, https://www.britannica.com/topic/millennial.
24 Jeff Wallenfeldt, "Silent Generation," *Encyclopedia Britannica*, last updated February 28, 2025, https://www.britannica.com/topic/Silent-Generation.
25 Twenge, *Generations*, 75.
26 Ibid., 53–55.
27 YWCA Minneapolis, "Lessons Learned from the Silent Generation," *Our Voices* (blog), February 28, 2017, https://www.ywcampls.org/blog-content/all-our-voices-blog/lessons-learned-from-the-silent-generation.
28 Twenge, *Generations*, 55, 60.

29 Seemiller and Grace, *Generation Z*, 6.
30 Bullinger, *Reagan's "Boys,"* 8.
31 Deborah L. Ruf, "Gifted Baby Boomers, How They Were Raised, and How They Raised You," SENG (Supporting Emotional Needs of the Gifted), March 14, 2023, https://www.sengifted.org/post/gifted-baby-boomers-how-they-were-raised-and-how-they-raised-you.
32 Twenge, *Generations*, 75.
33 Ibid., 82–83.
34 MTN Staff, "5 Brutal Truths About Who Had It Easier at 30—Boomers or Millennials?" MoneyTalksNews, February 10, 2025, https://www.moneytalksnews.com/slideshows/brutal-truths-about-who-had-it-easier-at-boomers-or-millennials/
35 Twenge, *Generations*, 91.
36 David Beren, "Baby Boomers Are Ditching the 9-to-5 Grind for Good," 24/7 Wall St., December 10, 2024, https://247wallst.com/personal-finance/2024/12/10/baby-boomers-are-ditching-the-9-to-5-grind-for-good/.
37 "Generation X (1965–1980)," Generation Check, accessed June 12, 2025, https://generationcheck.com/generations/generation-x; Patrick Kiger, "Boomers Once Led the World in Education. What Happened?" AARP, June 19, 2013, https://blog.aarp.org/bulletin-today/u-s-global-education-rankings-slipping-boomers-once-held-strong-lead.
38 Twenge, *Generations*, 136.
39 Thom S. Rainer, *The Millennials* (Nashville: B&H Publishing, 2011), 16.
40 "Baby Boomers: The Gloomiest Generation," Pew Research Center, June 25, 2008, https://www.pewresearch.org/social-trends/2008/06/25/baby-boomers-the-gloomiest-generation/.
41 "Audience Profile: Baby Boomers," Media Culture, May 26, 2023, https://www.mediaculture.com/insights/profile-baby-boomers.
42 "What Are Baby Boomers?" AllVoices, accessed June 12, 2025, https://www.allvoices.co/glossary/baby-boomers.
43 "Audience Profile: Baby Boomers."
44 Robert Tanner, "15 Influential Events That Shaped Generation X," Management Is a Journey, updated February 8, 2025, https://managementisajourney.com/fascinating-numbers-15-influential-events-that-shaped-generation-x/.
45 Seemiller and Grace, *Generation Z*, 7–8.
46 "The Digitally Savvy Generation: How Gen X Embraces Technology," Media Culture, December 15, 2023, https://www.mediaculture.com/insights/digitally-savvy-generation-how-gen-x-embraces-technology.
47 Twenge, *Generations*, 233.
48 "Generation X (1965–1980)."
49 Ibid.
50 Zelazko, "Millennial."
51 Ibid.

52 Twenge, *Generations*, 265.
53 "What Is Gentle Parenting?" Cleveland Clinic Health Essentials, August 5, 2022, https://health.clevelandclinic.org/what-is-gentle-parenting
54 Polly Dunbar, "'Gentle Parenting' Is No Way to Bring Up Children—and I Should Know," *Independent*, December 29, 2023, https://www.independent.co.uk/voices/gentle-parenting-millennials-parenting-gen-alpha-saying-no-emotions-b2468450.html.
55 Alexandra Blogier, "11 Benefits of Soft Parenting That Boomers Totally Disagree With," YourTango, December 3, 2024, https://www.yourtango.com/family/benefits-soft-parenting-boomers-totally-disagree.
56 Twenge, *Generations*, 247–48.

3 **Getting to Know Them**
Understanding Generation Z

Up to this point, we've explored the generations of the twentieth century. Now, we turn to the heart of this book: Generation Z and Generation Alpha. Each generation builds on the legacy of those before it, so understanding the past provides valuable insight into the traits and experiences that define these newer cohorts. Every generation is shaped by its own unique characteristics and the cultural events it collectively experiences. Generations Z and Alpha are coming of age in an era unlike any before, bringing with them distinct nuances, strengths, and challenges that reflect the unprecedented nature of their time.

The previous generation, commonly known as the millennials, or Generation Y, were once in the spotlight for their unique traits and quirky habits. They have now blended into the workforce, and Generation Z (aka Gen Z, iGen, and postmillennial), those born between 1995 and 2009, has become the focus of educational journals, marketing strategies, and workplace discussions.[1] As with any generation, there are both positive and negative opinions, along with a curiosity about the traits that may appear unique compared to other generations. Conversations about this group range from their obsession with the 1990s grunge aesthetic to how they rely on TikTok for important information. So just who is Generation Z? It is crucial to study the landscape of their upbringing and events that shaped them in order to understand them. Members of Gen Z witnessed the exponential growth of the internet, an array of culturally shifting events, and changing views on such issues as mental health awareness.

Technology

Born during the dot-com boom, Gen Z has experienced remarkable technological advancements throughout their lives. While Gen Zers may remember using clunky, gray CRT monitors during their daily computer time as children, which nowadays seem like ancient technology, they still do know a time without the internet. The oldest Gen Zers were born three years after the internet had been made public. Thus, members of Gen Z are known as digital natives because technology was an integral part of their upbringing. Using a computer mouse, uploading and downloading files, and ultimately knowing how to effortlessly carry out any task on the computer was and is a normal part of Gen Zers' lives. Not only did Gen Z experience the explosion of the internet and computers, but also the first iPhone was introduced in 2007 and was a major event that transformed mobile-device usage.[2] For many members of Gen Z, they would likely be more familiar with smartphones than such alternatives as landlines or flip phones.

Alongside smart devices, YouTube (2005) created the opportunity for endless, on-demand video streaming. Spotify (2008), iTunes (2001), and Apple Music (2015) provided unlimited music streaming in a manner like never before. During Gen Z's childhood, video calls had also become accessible thanks to video-conferencing tools like Skype (2003) and Windows Live Messenger (2006). Video calling became even more convenient with the creation of FaceTime in 2010. Gen Z also observed the global rise of video conference calls in professional settings during and after the 2020 pandemic. The latest technological advancement that Gen Z is navigating in the mid-2020s is artificial intelligence (AI), whose revolution has been compared to that of electricity.[3] Not surprisingly, the members of Gen Z are saturated with technology and, as digital natives, know how to efficiently use all these tools to their advantage. Gen Zers have been reported to spend five or more hours a day using their smart devices for entertainment purposes.[4] Users easily spend copious amounts of time on such social media platforms as Instagram, Tik Tok, and Snapchat. Unlike previous generations, Gen Z does not understand the concept of logging off, as they are always "on."[5]

Influential Events

Throughout any generation's upbringing, there have been historical events that have shifted views and culture. Generation Z has received their fair share, if not more, of major events that have caused change and unrest. September 11, 2001, scarred the United States, as it was the first time the homeland was attacked in such a way by an outside enemy. The ramifications include a more somber outlook on the country's sense of peace as well as a permanent change to airport security.[6] Gen Zers born before 9/11 would have been very young, and while they would have limited memories of this tragic event, they would have witnessed the fearful conversations and the new precautions that took place as a result. Gen Z would have also been in a similar position during the war in Afghanistan, the conflict that started in 2001, as well as the Great Recession of 2007–2009. While they were not old enough to take action in these times, Gen Z would have been surrounded by the anxiety and uncertainty their parents faced.

Gen Z also witnessed political events that shaped history, such as the 2008 election of Barack Obama as the first Black president of the United States, and the legalization of same-sex marriage in 2015. As Gen Z began to understand more of the world around them, political unrest in the United States became increasingly prominent. The 2016 and 2020 elections sadly carried with them divisive rhetoric, strained relationships, and at times behavior that led to legal consequences. Starting in March 2020, the global health crisis of the COVID-19 pandemic contributed to a further political divide in the United States, while the rest of the world was also suffering from deaths and broken economies. It was at this time that members of Generation Z became active in the political scene and participated in protests, petitions, and awareness

Technology	Influential Events
Internet (1993)	9/11 (2001)
Skype (2003), Windows Live Messenger (2006), and Facetime (2010)	War in Afghanistan (2001-21)
YouTube (2005)	Great Recession (2007-09)
iPhone (2007)	Election of First Black President (2008)
iTunes (2001), Spotify (2008), Apple Music (2015)	COVID-19 Pandemic (2020)

Figure 3.1 Gen Z technology and influential events. *Illustration by the author.*

campaigns. Additional events that added stress and chaos to the already-shaky American climate include the Black Lives Matter movement, Supreme Court decisions, and the historically challenging economic situation.[7]

Mental Health Awareness

Amid global challenges, Gen Z has experienced growing levels of distress, prompting a deeper and more widespread interest in mental health. Arthur Evans, CEO of the American Psychological Association, stated, "Current events are clearly stressful for everyone in the country, but young people are really feeling the impact of issues in the news, particularly those issues that may feel beyond their control."[8] Surveys conducted on the mental health of Gen Z confirmed what many were thinking: The mental health of young people was at an all-time low, creating an alarming issue that needed to be addressed. In the early 2020s, the American Academy of Pediatrics and the American Academy of Child and Adolescent Psychiatry announced a national emergency concerning the mental health of children and adolescents.[9]

In addition to the state of the world causing anxiety for young people, the previously unexplored extreme addiction to technology did not help matters when it came to the mental health of Gen Z. During the pandemic lockdown, digital usage reached new highs, and some were using their screens 17.5 hours a day.[10] The hours that Gen Z spent on their smart devices sometimes served as an escape from reality but also may have been detrimental. The research on the effects of heavy technology usage on brain development and overall wellness is still new. However, one can surmise from both common sense and from emerging articles that overuse of screens for such activities as doomscrolling (spending excessive amounts of time online scrolling through content that is not necessarily productive) cannot be beneficial.[11] Lakshmi Kannan and T. P. Kumar assert,

> *Being socially connected to others can ease stress, anxiety, and depression, boost self-worth, provide comfort and joy, and prevent loneliness. . . . Everyone is different and there is no specific amount of time spent on social media and no one can control the time one spends over social sites or the frequency one checks for updates, or the number of posts one makes and likes but these don't indicate by any means that the user is being unhealthy, but if this excess use causes one to neglect face-to-face relationships and the society, causes distractions at work [sic] school, or is developing feelings of envy, hatred, or*

one is posting pictures to show others or make others jealous, its [sic] time one thinks and relooks into their social behavior and social media habits.[12]

A more recent development in the evolving landscape of technology is the emergence of generative AI. Generative AI (gen AI) can create new content by "learning" from a large database.[13] Gen AI quickly took over the internet after the publicly accessible ChatGPT site was introduced in November 2022.[14] While gen AI is beneficial in many capacities and has proven to be a worthy tool, it can cause more chaos in the digital realm. Because gen AI is becoming so widely used and is improving daily, it is becoming more difficult to distinguish between authentic and fabricated material. Not only is there an overabundance of information on the web, but now there is also the worry of determining the validity of posts, reels, stories, memes, and other content we have become accustomed to seeing.[15]

Due to the amplified need for mental health services, more resources have been made available on BetterHelp and other platforms where one can meet with a therapist online.[16] It is a rather ironic twist that the same technology that has contributed to the mental health crisis is also a potential source for solutions. There is also an abundance of apps that assist with wellness and self-help. Even though social media may have contributed to the need for mental health services, mental health awareness is promoted through such platforms as Instagram and TikTok.[17]

Education

In education, Gen Z is generally known for displaying self-reliance and flexibility. Individuals from this generation would have been in elementary school through college when COVID-19 forced students to use heightened resourcefulness frequently during online learning and restricted in-person interactions and meetings. If a student could not figure out the answer to a problem, they became adept at discovering information on their own. Gen Z also became more flexible during the pandemic, resulting in more comfort with hybrid learning, asynchronous learning, online lectures, video submissions, and a wide variety of other educational formats.[18] Not only are Gen Z students multimodal regarding their favored pedagogical strategies, but they also like to learn through all five senses and prefer active, hands-on learning, as they are practical and pragmatic in their thinking.[19]

As a result of the unique COVID-19 education situation, Gen Z students do not rely on the teacher as the sole source of information. The average Gen Z student knows how to conduct a proper internet search and can find information from scholarly journals and even TikTok videos. Gen Z also uses YouTube, Google, and such AI tools as CoPilot and ChatGPT to learn. In spite of the obstacles COVID-19 threw in their way, Gen Z students are ambitious and want to perform at a high level. Unlike the millennial trend of participation trophies, Gen Z understands the value of competition and respects fair play.[20]

Gen Z is also open to learning about other cultures and is diversity driven. Perhaps due to today's global nature of the world, with the sharing of news and other content on the same social media platforms, it is easier for Gen Z students to feel more connected and think similarly even across continents. Today's Gen Z student is more open than previous generations to learning about other cultures and studying disparities and resemblances.[21]

Due to increased uses of technology and the culture of immediate results, Gen Z displays shorter attention spans.[22] In fact, the average attention span has decreased from 12 seconds to 8.5 seconds over the past two decades—putting humans a half-second behind goldfish, who have an attention span of 9 seconds.[23] Similarly, Gen Z is driven by instant gratification, and they want to see a result minutes after the initial thought.[24] In a world where meal and snack delivery companies like Uber Eats, Gopuff, DoorDash, and others can offer food at just the tap of a button, the growing desire for instant gratification makes sense.

As mental health challenges are increasingly common among Generation Z, such conditions as anxiety and depression are often observed in student populations. Many Gen Z students are aware of the importance of mental well-being in today's world and actively work on prioritizing this aspect of their health. Such studies as S. G. Deanda's found that after the COVID-19 pandemic, Gen Z students are showing an increased need for mental health awareness, support systems, and easy access to mental health resources.[25] Music students in particular display a concerning struggle with mental health, as has been concluded by many recent studies. One study on undergraduate music-education students labeled their responses about their mental health as "code red," meaning they used "emotionally charged, extreme, or desperate language."[26]

Social Life and Communication

Gen Z loves global collaboration as well as learning about other cultures and displays a greater appreciation for diversity.[27] Because of the ease of communicating with anyone in the world through advances in technology, Gen Z often has contact with those in other countries through direct communication or commenting on the content of creators across borders. Senge states, "Young people around the world are creating a web of relationships that has never existed before."[28] Gen Z loves to talk with others through social media platforms, and as other generations before them, they use slang to communicate ideas or express a thought.[29]

During the COVID and post-COVID eras, Gen Zers were sometimes hesitant to talk with others, but as the world has recovered, many prefer to converse in person and are perhaps realizing the value of in-person interactions and memories made from those interactions.[30] In a 2024 study, results showed that 77 percent of Gen Z participants liked in-person conversation, 54 percent of participants liked text messaging, and 47 percent of participants liked the modality of direct messaging (messages sent through a social media platform such as Facebook or Instagram).[31] Even if an introverted Gen Zer may not lean toward in-person interactions over digital ones, they still appreciate the efficiency and ability to express emotion in person. Gen Z even desires to find love the old-fashioned way, in a grocery store or at an event.[32] While Gen Z prefers in-person communication, they might lack some of the skills needed for a successful in-person conversation. All the time spent online can dampen social skills.[33]

The Workforce

Because many members of Gen Z are in the workforce, it is useful to briefly discuss them in this setting, as there is a good chance that they may currently be our employees, teaching assistants, or coworkers. Gen Z workers are known to have prioritized work-life balance more and practice self-care.[34] Self-care initiatives that Gen Z has engaged in include nutritional wellness, such as advocating for whole foods, and unplugging from work when they are off the clock.[35]

Gen Z employees prefer nonhierarchical leadership and will likely be bolder compared to other generations in questioning authority and asking for justification about rules. They are also used to finding information on their own, so dealing with authority figures may be difficult for them in some situations. Gen Z employees tend to be practical, so engaging them in constructive dialogue that explains the purpose behind certain functions or traditions can be especially effective.[36] Gen Z employees, like students, remain positive toward hybrid work and are comfortable working from home.[37]

Summary of Gen Z Traits

In Education

- Exhibit self-reliance and flexibility as learners, shaped by the pandemic
- Demonstrate comfort with hybrid, online, and multimodal learning formats
- Prefer hands-on, sensory-rich learning
- Are practical and results-focused
- Leverage such tools as Google, YouTube, ChatGPT, and TikTok effectively to access information
- Value achievement and fair competition over participation trophies
- Reflect a globally oriented mindset and respect for other cultures and perspectives
- Have shorter attention spans and seek instant results
- Prioritize mental health
- Often face anxiety and stress, especially those in music studies

In Social Life and Communication

- Embrace global connection through social media
- Prefer in-person interaction but may lack strong face-to-face skills
- Communicate with slang
- Value emotional expression
- Interested in authentic, old-fashioned ways of connecting

In the Workforce

- Prioritize work-life balance and self-care
- Prefer collaborative, nonhierarchical environments
- Question rules and seek purpose behind expectations
- Are independent and comfortable with remote or hybrid work

Gen Z in Today's World

Challenges

The perfect storm of obsessive technological usage and addiction has created the illusion of unrealistic lifestyles on social media. This has contributed to an unstable national and global atmosphere, with Gen Z finding itself in a mental health epidemic. Sadly, many teenagers and young adults struggle with depression and anxiety.[38] Gen Z also tends to question authority and challenge long-standing norms. While it is sometimes met with resistance, this trait often reflects critical thinking, a desire for progress, and a willingness to reconstruct outdated systems. Additionally, Gen Z's social interactions may be hampered and underdeveloped due to isolation during the pandemic years as well as more time with technology, which often results in less time engaging in human interaction. This generation struggles with a short attention span and a need for instant gratification, which can hinder their ability to focus deeply, to engage in sustained problem-solving, and to complete long-term goals. In academic and professional settings, this may lead to difficulties with concentration; reduced productivity; and a preference for quick fixes over thoughtful, strategic planning. Over time, this can affect learning, creativity, and the development of resilience in the face of complex challenges.

In a Nutshell: Challenges of Gen Z

- **Mental Health Struggles:** High rates of depression and anxiety contribute to a broader mental health epidemic. Social media fosters unrealistic lifestyle comparisons and self-esteem issues.
- **Disrupted Social Development:** Pandemic-related isolation and excessive screen time have hindered in-person social skills. Reduced face-to-face interaction may lead to underdeveloped interpersonal communication.

- **Short Attention Span:** Preference for instant gratification affects focus and deep engagement. There is difficulty with sustained problem-solving and long-term goal completion.
- **Challenges in Academic and Professional Settings:** Reduced productivity and concentration and a tendency to seek quick fixes over strategic, long-term planning potentially affect creativity and resilience.
- **Authority Skepticism:** A tendency to question norms and challenge authority can be both a strength and a source of conflict.

Strengths

While the excessive use of technology may have brought about some negative effects, it has also introduced many benefits, including the opportunity to connect with others around the world and learn about other cultures. Consequently, Gen Z is a culturally aware generation and is open to change and diversity. Another benefit stemming from a life of technology is that those born after 1994 are more than likely very tech savvy—they can come up with creative solutions for tech-related challenges and are fluent with digital tools.

Members of Generation Z are pragmatic and innovative thinkers. They are also quick learners. They can see a trend or useful idea on the internet, take in what they need, and apply it to their lives. As well as being a quick learner, the typical Gen Z student is self-directed and will not sit around waiting to be told what to do, especially if they are already self-motivated. Overall, members of Gen Z are sharp, capable, digitally skilled go-getters who will continue to learn and improve the world as they go.

In a Nutshell: Strengths of Gen Z

- **Cultural Awareness and Openness:** They embrace diversity and inclusivity across cultures, races, and identities and are open to change and progressive values.
- **Technological Fluency:** Highly tech savvy and comfortable with digital tools, they are capable of solving tech-related problems creatively.
- **Innovative and Pragmatic Thinking:** They are quick to learn and adapt to new trends or ideas and are able to apply online knowledge practically in real life.

- **Self-Directed Learning:** Independent and proactive learners, they are motivated to seek out knowledge and solutions without waiting for instruction.
- **Global Connectivity:** They use technology to connect with people and ideas worldwide, building a broader worldview through digital interaction.
- **Resilient and Capable:** Despite challenges, Gen Z continues to grow, learn, and strive to improve the world.

Where Do We Go from Here?

Piano teachers have a unique opportunity not only to gift Gen Z with the lifelong skill of playing the piano as a form of self-care but also to guide them through the entire journey of a project. In doing so, they help instill the understanding that with planning, logical thinking, and determination, even the most daunting tasks can be accomplished. Gen Z, along with every person who has come before them, just wants to be understood.

Notes

1. José Magano, Cláudia Silva, Cláudia Figueiredo, Andreia Vitória, Teresa Nogueira, and Maria Alzira Pimenta Dinis, "Generation Z: Fitting Project Management Soft Skills Competencies—A Mixed-Method Approach," *Education Sciences* 10, no. 7 (July 2020): 187, https://doi.org/10.3390/educsci10070187.
2. Alison Eldridge, "Generation Z," *Encyclopaedia Britannica*, updated October 9, 2025, https://www.britannica.com/topic/Generation-Z; "Generation Z at School," McCrindle, accessed October 9, 2025, https://mccrindle.com.au/article/generation-z-at-school/.
3. Cecilia Ka Yuk Chan and Katherine K. W. Lee, "The AI Generation Gap: Are Gen Z Students More Interested in Adopting Generative AI Such as ChatGPT in Teaching and Learning than Their Gen X and Millennial Generation Teachers?" *Smart Learning Environments* 10, no. 60 (2023): 2–3, https://doi.org/10.1186/s40561-023-00269-3; Kyle Orland, "Is Generative AI Really Going to Wreak Havoc on the Power Grid?" *Ars Technica*, June 25, 2024, https://arstechnica.com/ai/2024/06/is-generative-ai-really-going-to-wreak-havoc-on-the-power-grid/.
4. Peter Brown, "Trends in Gen Z Smartphone Habits," Electronics360, January 19, 2024, https://electronics360.globalspec.com/article/20639/trends-in-gen-z-smartphone-habits.

5   Juliet Milillo, "Wellness Awakening: Gen Z as the Catalyst for a Well-Being Revolution" (master's thesis, Liberty University, 2024), 26, https://digitalcommons.liberty.edu/masters/1202/.

6   Janet Bednarek, "How 9/11 Transformed Airport Security," World Economic Forum, September 8, 2021, https://www.weforum.org/stories/2021/09/how-9-11-transformed-airport-security/.

7   Stella Sechopoulos, "Do Young Adults in the US Have It Harder than Their Parents?" World Economic Forum, March 10, 2022, https://www.weforum.org/stories/2022/03/young-adults-future-finance-housing-inflation/.

8   Cited in Sophie Bethune, "Gen Z More Likely to Report Mental Health Concerns," *Monitor on Psychology* 50, no. 1 (January 2019): 20, https://www.apa.org/monitor/2019/01/gen-z.

9   Annie E. Casey Foundation, "Generation Z and Mental Health," *Casey Connects* (blog), updated May 12, 2024, https://www.aecf.org/blog/generation-z-and-mental-health.

10 Apurvakumar Pandya and Pragya Lodha, "Social Connectedness, Excessive Screen Time During COVID-19 and Mental Health: A Review of Current Evidence," *Frontiers in Human Dynamics* 3 (July 2021): 4, https://doi.org/10.3389/fhumd.2021.684137.

11 "Doomscroll," Merriam-Webster, accessed October 27, 2024, https://www.merriam-webster.com/dictionary/doomscroll.

12 Lakshmi Kannan and T. P. Kumar, "Social Media—The Emotional and Mental Roller-Coaster of Gen Z: An Empirical Study," in *Managing Disruptions in Business: Causes, Conflicts, and Controls*, ed. Rajagopal and Ramesh Behl, Palgrave Studies in Democracy, Innovation, and Entrepreneurship for Growth, 81–102 (Palgrave Macmillan, 2022), 81.

13 "Generative AI," Merriam-Webster, accessed October 27, 2024, https://www.merriam-webster.com/dictionary/generative%20AI.

14 "What Is Generative AI?" McKinsey and Company, April 2, 2024, https://www.mckinsey.com/featured-insights/mckinsey-explainers/what-is-generative-ai.

15 Nicole Summers-Gabr, Violeta Gutkowski, and Alice L. Kassens, "Gen Z's Mental Health, Economic Distress and Technology," *Open Vault* (blog), May 22, 2024, https://www.stlouisfed.org/open-vault/2024/may/gen-z-mental-health-economic-distress-and-technology.

16 "About Us," BetterHelp, accessed October 27, 2024, https://www.betterhelp.com/about/.

17 "Useful Wellness and Mental Health Apps," UCSF Human Resources, accessed June 13, 2025, https://hr.ucsf.edu/wellbeing/coping-and-resiliency-program/cope-program-wellness-resources/useful-wellness-and-mental-health-apps.

18 Melissa De Witte, "What to Know About Gen Z," *Stanford Report*, January 3, 2022, https://news.stanford.edu/stories/2022/01/know-gen-z; Tali Te'eni Harari, Yaron Sela, and Liad Bareket-Bojmel, "Gen Z During the COVID-19 Crisis: A Comparative Analysis of the Differences Between Gen Z and Gen X in Resilience, Values and Attitudes," *Current Psychology* 42 (2023): 24223–32, https://doi.org/10.1007/s12144-022-03501-4.

19 Evangelin Whitehead, "Augmented Skills of Educators Teaching Generation Z," *Excellence in Education Journal* 12, no. 1 (Winter 2023): 32–54, https://files.eric.ed.gov/fulltext/EJ1366828.pdf.

20 Melody Morrison, "Gen Z and Gen Alpha: Who Are They and How Do We Teach Them?" *Florida Music Director* 77, no. 2 (2023): 26–31; Joel Stein, "Millennials: The Me Me Me Generation," *Time*, May 20, 2013, https://time.com/247/millennials-the-me-me-me-generation/.

21 Corey Seemiller, Meghan Grace, Paula Dal Bo Campagnolo, Isa Mara Da Rosa Alves, Gustavo Severo De Borba, "How Generation Z College Students Prefer to Learn: A Comparison of U.S. and Brazil Students," *Journal of Educational Research and Practice* 9, no. 1 (2019): 349–68, https://doi.org/10.5590/JERAP.2019.09.1.25.

22 Maribel Rachel Diz, "Gen Z and Millennials in the Workplace: How Are Leaders Adapting to Their Short Attention Span and How Will They Keep Them from Leaving? A Qualitative Study" (PhD diss., Florida International University, 2021), 38, https://digitalcommons.fiu.edu/etd/4800/.

23 "Average Human Attention Span (Statistics)," Golden Steps ABA, March 4, 2025, https://www.goldenstepsaba.com/resources/average-attention-span.

24 Whitehead, "Augmented Skills."

25 Steven G. Deanda, "A Phenomenological Study to Understand the Impact of COVID-19 on Mental Health Among Generation Z Pharmacy Students" (PhD diss., Texas A&M University–Kingsville, 2024), ProQuest, https://www.proquest.com/dissertations-theses/phenomenological-study-understand-impact-covid-19/docview/3059229386/se-2.

26 Lisa Huisman Koops and Christa R. Kuebel, "Self-Reported Mental Health and Mental Illness Among University Music Students in the United States," *Research Studies in Music Education* 43, no. 2 (July 2021): 129–43, https://doi.org/10.1177/1321103X19863265.

27 De Witte, "What to Know."

28 Peter Senge, *The Fifth Discipline: The Art and Practice of the Learning Organization* (Crown Business, 2010).

29 Eliza M. Jeresano and Marigrace D. Carretero, "Digital Culture and Social Media Slang of Gen Z," *United International Journal for Research and Technology* 3, no. 4 (2022): 11–25.

30 De Witte, "What to Know."

31 Shefaly Shorey, Daria Vyugina, Natalia Waechter, and Nina Dolev, "Communication Preferences and Behaviors," in *Gen Z Around the World: Understanding the Global Cohort Culture of Generation Z*, ed. Corey Seemiller and Meghan Grace, 31–42 (Emerald, 2024), 40, https://doi.org/10.1108/978-1-83797-092-620241004.

32 Asia Grace, "Gen Z Is Finding Love at a Surprising Place You Visit Often, Study Reveals," *New York Post*, October 24, 2024, https://nypost.com/2024/10/24/lifestyle/gen-z-is-finding-love-at-a-surprising-place-you-visit-often-study-reveals/; Coleby Phillips,

"'You Have to Adapt': New Study Reveals Gen Z Dating Preferences in Arizona," *Arizona Republic*, August 17, 2024, https://www.azcentral.com/story/news/local/arizona/2024/08/17/generation-z-daters-wish-to-sway-away-from-online-dating-study-shows/74707888007/.

33 Shorey et al., "Communication Preferences and Behaviors," 40.
34 Hassan Choughari, "The Impact of Gen Z in the Workplace," *Forbes*, February 5, 2024, https://www.forbes.com/councils/forbeshumanresourcescouncil/2024/02/05/the-impact-of-gen-z-in-the-workplace/.
35 Milillo, "Wellness Awakening," 34.
36 De Witte, "What to Know."
37 Harari, Sela, and Bareket-Bojmel, "Gen Z During COVID-19," 24225.
38 Bethune, "Gen Z More Likely."

4 Mapping Their World
Who Is Generation Alpha?

Members of Generation Alpha have been dubbed "iPad kids" by those who have observed their (sometimes) inseparable relationship with touchscreen tablets in grocery stores, church, doctors' offices—even the playground. Gen Alpha was born into a world entranced with the capabilities of smart devices, as the iPad was created in 2010, the year the first alpha babies were born. Instagram, the popular social media platform, was also introduced in 2010. Not surprisingly, the American Dialect Society voted *app* as the word of the year in 2010.[1] Generation Z grew up in an era already connected by digital devices and witnessed numerous technological breakthroughs. In contrast, Generation Alpha was born into an even more advanced digital landscape. Generation Alpha engages in app-based play and heavy video streaming, often from infancy, which has earned them the label an "unintentional global experiment."[2] Generation Alpha is the first to grow up with such intense exposure to technology from a young age, making it difficult to fully understand the potential benefits and drawbacks of being raised with smart devices and apps.

At the time of this publication, the oldest member of Generation Alpha is in high school, and the youngest member is not yet one year old. Consequently, there is little research conducted on this group compared to previous generations, and the distinguishing facts that differentiate them from others are still blurry. Members of Gen Alpha are still developing and becoming individuals with their own values and characteristics. As Generation Alpha's characteristics continue to emerge, experts use quantitative data alongside informed insights to make predictions.

Demographics and Other Facts

In December 2024, two billion Gen Alphas were roaming the earth, making them the largest generation in history.[3] In addition to being the biggest generation, Gen Alpha is also the most diverse in such countries as the United States and Canada. The 2020 US Census revealed that the diversity index (the chance that two people chosen at random are from different racial and ethnic groups) is 68.4 percent for children ages five through seventeen. Additionally, the diversity index for children under age five is 69 percent.[4]

Generation Alpha has unprecedented access to information, allowing them to look up any topic instantly. Imagine walking down the street in the 1920s and telling someone that their great-great-grandchild could, with a few taps on a device, learn about the signing of the Declaration of Independence, view original documents, and watch expert videos within minutes. In just a century, we have seen advancements that were once unimaginable. This easy access to information ensures that Generation Alpha will drive exciting developments and bring greater efficiency and benefits to humanity.

What We Have Observed So Far . . .

According to a 2020 study, Generation Alpha is characterized by higher curiosity, mobility, self-centeredness, and emotional awareness compared to Generation Z, along with a tendency to be more rule-free and ill-tempered. They also exhibit higher self-esteem and more individualistic communication, leading preschool teachers to adopt reconstructive classroom-management techniques for them, unlike the more traditional methods used for Generation Z.[5]

We can also infer that Generation Alpha's socioeconomic development differs from previous generations, as they reportedly spend seven to eight hours a day on screens, with nearly every aspect of their lives embedded in the digital world.[6] While hampered social development is an obvious issue that must be addressed, there are undeniably new benefits from this increased digital literacy. Coding used to require years of schooling and certification, but Generation Alpha already is exploring this realm of technology. In fact, Gen Alpha is learning such coding languages as Java and Python in elementary schools.[7] Members of Generation Alpha are not only experts at using the current technology but are branching beyond mere usage and into the creation of digital functions.[8] While Gen Z adapted to digital tools during their school years, Gen Alpha has never known a world without them. This difference has led to a shift in classroom-management styles, with Gen Z responding to structured routines and Gen Alpha requiring more adaptive, student-led learning environments

Summary

Again, Generation Alpha is a fascinating and exciting mystery, with much more data and insights to be uncovered in the coming years. We know for certain that this generation is the biggest and most diverse in history. We know that Gen Alpha spends its formative years in app-based play and watching content online. We are also aware that children of today have decreased attention spans and increased digital literacy. Studies have concluded that this escalated screen time has resulted in weaker social skills and development. The key takeaway from this analysis of Generation Alpha is that, more than ever, adult guidance is crucial in shaping the next generation into productive, happy, and fulfilled individuals.

Technology

Generation Alpha, much like Generation Z, has grown up surrounded by digital devices. However, Gen Alpha has experienced an even deeper immersion in tech from an early age. For them, digital tools are not just a convenience but also an integral part of everyday life.[9]

Apple technology that has emerged during Gen Alpha's lifetime includes the iPad (2010), Apple Watch (2014), and AirPods (2016). Their invention inspired other brands, making smart tablets, smart watches, and wireless earbuds even more popular. Other digital tools that have appeared in the modern household include the smart speaker (2015) and virtual reality headset, which has had a lengthy history but was made popular for household use in 2019.[10]

Most everyday activities that Gen Alpha children engage in are different from those of the past because there is now emphasis on the digital world of the future. Even toys are now made to teach young children how to code in languages like Python and JavaScript.[11] Anki's Cozmo Robot uses AI to mimic human behavior and teach children to code in an interactive way.[12] In addition to Cozmo Robot, there are many other robots and toys that offer screen-free coding training and practice.[13] Even babies often play with toy cell phones that mimic apps and video calls on the "screen."

There are many replacements for the tools used just a few years ago. Instead of MSN Messenger for exchanging fun instant messages with friends, Gen Alphas use texting and Snapchat.[14] In past years, if someone wanted to receive advice on a topic or niche interest, they would likely speak with a trusted friend or family member or go to someone they knew could offer helpful guidance. In the twenty-first century, people turned to Google and Reddit for learning and advice, finding them to be reliable sources of information and support. Nowadays, it is perhaps more common to receive counsel from TikTok, YouTube, or ChatGPT on a particular subject. After all, if an influencer is saying this, then it must be true, right?

Similarly, while news was once primarily consumed through TV, newspapers, and online articles, younger people today get their news differently. Again, TikTok, YouTube, and even Snapchat are primary sources of information for world events. These platforms typically provide concise news summaries, highlighting key points and presenting the story in a visually engaging manner that keeps viewers' attention[15] Unlike Gen Z, many of whom transitioned from analog to digital during their formative years, Gen Alpha was born into a fully digital world. For Gen Z, smartphones were a novelty in middle school; for Gen Alpha, they're a default toy in preschool. See table 4.1, which lists some of the most influential technology that Generation Alpha uses.

Artificial Intelligence

The concept of artificial intelligence (AI) is not new. AI got its start in 1956, with ideas and prototypes created along the way. AI was used for machine chess matches and speech recognition. Language learning was another innovative branch of this technology. Eventually Siri and Google Assistant, based on machine learning, natural language processing, and voice recognition, were developed.

During Generation Alpha's lifetime, one of the biggest technological advancements has been the rise of deep learning, a type of AI.[16] Deep learning uses complex algorithms called neural networks that work similarly to the human brain. These networks study large amounts of data, like text, pictures, and sounds, to recognize patterns and make predictions. Smart speakers, such as Amazon Echo, Apple HomePod, and Google Home, are examples of deep-learning devices.

Deep-learning technology has become the foundation for generative AI, which can create new content instead of just analyzing it. For example, generative AI can write stories, create pictures, compose music, and even

Table 4.1 Core Technologies Defining the Gen Alpha Experience

Tablets	iPad (2010) Samsung Galaxy Tab (2010)
Smart Homes	Smart Thermostat (2007) Amazon Echo (2014) Google Home (2016)
AI	Google Assistant (2006) Siri (2011) Amazon Echo (2014) DALL-E (2021) ChatGPT (2022) CoPilot (2023) Gemini (2023)
Streaming Platforms	Hulu (2007) Netflix (2007) Disney+ (2019)
Video Content	Twitch (2011) TikTok (2016) Instagram Reels (2020) YouTube Shorts (2020)
Wearable Tech	Fitbit (2009) Oculus Rift (2013) Apple Watch (2015) Samsung Watch (2018) Meta Quest (2023)

draw realistic human faces. Generative AI does this by learning from existing examples and then producing new, similar content. OpenAI's user-friendly ChatGPT and DALL-E opened the door for the public to experience the wonders of this new technological advancement. With the rapid takeover of AI tools, major tech firms like Microsoft, Google, Apple, Amazon, and Meta have quickly hurried to integrate AI into their products.[17]

Generative AI has become a significant part of the technological landscape that Generation Alpha is growing up with. While AI has opened many creative options and will continue to offer many more wonderful possibilities, there are also concerns of copyright issues, education and business ethics, and lack of creativity and critical thinking, as AI can often quickly solve day-to-day problems and create original content with just a simple prompt. The world has yet to witness the full capacity of AI, and Generation Alpha will have a front-row seat to watch it all unfold.

Online Gaming: Gen Alpha's New Social Media

While Gen Z is reported to spend 23 percent of their leisure time on social media and 17 percent engaged in gaming, Gen Alpha kids and teens devote 21 percent of their leisure time to gaming, making it their primary source of entertainment.[18] Millennials fondly remember when social media was a place for genuine interactions with family and friends. However, this has changed significantly, with timelines now dominated by ads, influencer promotions, and polished content, leading to a sense of disconnect from the authentic social experiences of the past.

In response, many Gen Alphas are turning to gaming platforms. These virtual spaces not only provide entertainment but also foster a sense of community and connection that traditional social media now struggles to offer. While the original social media platforms still have their place, this younger generation is finding deeper engagement and meaningful interactions in these digital environments. One of the dominant online hangouts for Gen Alpha kids is the user-centered generated (UCG) game *Roblox*.[19] In this virtual world, players can create their own content, allowing room for self-expression and creativity, with the ability to share these products with their friends. Think of the days when kids would make mud pies and build pillow forts. This contains some of the same elements but is all contained in a digital environment. A few more popular games Gen Alphas enjoy playing together are *Fortnite, Among Us,* and *Minecraft*. While Gen Z's social lives were shaped by platforms like Instagram and Snapchat, Gen Alpha is forging friendships in virtual worlds like *Roblox* and *Minecraft*. This shift reflects a broader trend toward interactive, co-creative digital spaces.

Influential Events

Just as with Gen Z, Gen Alpha experiences different living conditions and cultural impacts in its upbringing when compared to previous generations, such as the inflation crisis that began in 2021 and present-day social justice and environmental movements. The characteristics that distinguish Generation Alpha from earlier generations will continue to shape its unique identity and to create common traits among its members.[20]

COVID-19

One influential event that occurred in Generation Alpha's time was the COVID-19 pandemic. Generation Alpha experienced this differently than Generation Z, as their formative years for social and emotional development were disrupted for a time. This was the first time any living person had experienced entire cities shut down and businesses empty. Overnight, schools, government buildings, stores, and nearly every establishment were forced to transfer to a virtual method to carry out day-to-day operations. Public transportation was thrown into mass chaos as the world entered a new normal. Many parents who usually sent their kids to school had to now work from home while trying to ensure that online school was progressing smoothly.

Many Gen Alphas were in foundational years of elementary school and were forced to miss out on social and scholastic development, as they were not allowed to physically attend school for months.[21] Educators say that while students were negatively affected by the pandemic, they do see improvements in behavior and social skills the more time goes on.[22] Many Gen Alphas who are old enough to remember their elementary school years on Zoom are grateful for the in-person interaction that is once again normalized today. Fortunately, a few years after the global crisis, other younger Gen Alphas either barely remember it or were not yet born, but they will likely always hear about the worldwide shutdown that affected their families.[23]

Family Dynamics

Many millennial parents of Generation Alpha children are moving away from traditional family-raising methods. This shift is partly deliberate and, to a certain degree, a result of changing circumstances. Within many Gen Alpha households, both parents are working and must establish a work-life balance as they move away from traditional gender roles to run a household. While this is not new, the decline of the traditional nuclear family has continued as economies, priorities, and perspectives change. Additionally, families are more likely to be blended, with divorces and remarriages more common than in the past.[24] While all this may be chaotic for a child at times, it teaches them resiliency and adaptability.[25]

Despite the busy schedules of today, millennial parents are choosing to prioritize time with their children as much as they can. Emotional well-being and maturity are also discussed and implemented more in today's household. This may be partly due to millennial parents choosing to have children later in life, resulting in an older average age of parents compared to previous generations. In the past, it used to be common to have a twenty- to twenty-five-year gap between generations. However, couples wait longer now to have children due to economic or societal changes or merely because they want to ensure that they are truly ready to raise a child.[26] Along with exposure to diverse family structures and environments, advancements in medicine and health care mean people are living longer, giving today's children more opportunities to interact with multiple generations.

Education

As mentioned previously, online games are a large part of Gen Alpha's childhood playtime and social experiences. Thus, gamification in Gen Alpha education is important and will prove effective for young learners. Pumudu Fernando and Salinda Premadasa state that technology and game-based pedagogical approaches "significantly impact the primary education process compared to traditional teaching methods."[27] Both digital and nondigital games increase interest and curiosity throughout the learning process. While there are different approaches to gamification, such as incorporating game elements like points, levels, and badges or fully converting learning materials into a game, students have responded positively to all gamification in their learning. The only thing that occasionally holds them back is losing motivation when the leaderboard shows they aren't performing well. Though gamification is present in education, there is still a need for more innovative and adaptive approaches.[28] Successful approaches to gamification are discussed in chapters 5 and 9.

Technology and societal changes have caused a major shift in education.[29] Gen Z had to adjust to digital learning tools as they emerged, often using them as supplements to traditional methods. In contrast, Gen Alpha expects technology to be seamlessly integrated into their learning experience, with personalized, gamified, and AI-enhanced instruction as the norm. Teachers must provide engaging, visual, multimodal, and hands-on methods to effectively teach these young Gen Alpha students.[30] Students already tend to be generally less engaged in the learning process, and this trend appears even more pronounced among Generation Alpha, who are growing up in a fast-paced, digitally saturated environment.[31]

Middle school educator Jessica Kato states that in order to effectively spark learning in Generation Alpha students, we need to find what genuinely engages their curiosity and connects with their lived experiences.[32] Gen Alpha students appreciate global connection and sharing digital content, so one idea is to assign projects where they can create something that they can share with others. Another approach is to let students select some of the content they learn or decide how the material is presented in class. In addition to highly engaging teaching, students expect teachers to customize their learning to their individual needs and preferences. They are not keen on the "one size fits all" classroom experience but instead seek highly individualized learning that reflects their interests, strengths, and preferred modes of engagement.[33] Adaptive learning technologies that tailor content to a student's progress are particularly effective for today's learners. Education consultants encourage teachers to "develop personalized learning pathways that align with their technological fluency and individual interests."[34]

While students are seemingly more independent as they are fully adept at the technology they use to study and learn, the value of parental support and involvement is just as crucial as ever. An educational mobile app may substitute for a parent in drilling their child with flash cards, but it will not provide the emotional support and motivation a child requires for full success and accountability in their endeavors.[35]

AI cannot be left off the table when discussing any level of education after 2022. The use of AI in education has raised significant ethical dilemmas, as students can exploit generative AI tools to cheat and bypass the need for critical thinking and creativity. Additionally, there are concerns about misinformation, and educational systems and tests must be overhauled to account for AI capabilities. Teachers must ensure that their students are engaging in critical thinking and developing their ability to produce original work and cultivate unique ideas. Despite the concerns that are raised when AI steps into the world of education, it can be used for good and has more potential benefits for learning than it has drawbacks.[36]

Summary of Gen Alpha Traits

In Education

- Engages readily with gamification (points, levels, badges, games), boosting curiosity
- Expect tech fully integrated, with personalized, adaptive, and AI-enhanced learning
- Prefer interactive, visual, hands-on, and relevant teaching methods
- Value creating and sharing digital projects globally
- Reject "one size fits all" in favor of learning tailored to interests and strengths
- Still need parental support for motivation and emotional growth
- Receive benefits from AI but require focus on critical thinking and original work

In Social Life and Communication

- Socialize in digital/virtual spaces (gaming platforms like *Roblox*, *Fortnite*)
- Communicate with fast, visual, multimodal (videos, emojis, short clips) forms
- Prefer interactive, co-creative platforms over traditional social media
- Favor concise, dynamic interaction due to shorter attention spans
- Need adult guidance to develop social and emotional skills

Gen Alpha in Today's World

Challenges

As has been the case with past generations, many kids are growing up with less parental involvement, as both parents are often working. Additionally, Generation Alpha is growing up amid rapid technological advancement, which can target young viewers with inappropriate content that may contradict what they are being taught. Many Gen Alphas say they trust their favorite social media influencers as much as they trust their own family members.[37] Tweens, children between the ages of eight and twelve, are seen as their own demographic, targeted by ad companies as a consumer segment. This demonstrates the "up-ageing" of tweens, indicating that the period of true childhood is shorter than it used to be because of unlimited access to technology and outside influences.[38]

In addition to the fact that Gen Alpha is growing up too quickly, there are fears of increased schadenfreude (pleasure in response to another's misfortune). Three neuroscientists write that Gen Alpha's constant exposure to violent or tragic content—often framed humorously on platforms like TikTok or YouTube—may foster a blunted emotional response to real-world suffering.[39] Dehumanization can occur while interacting only through screens and becoming desensitized to seeing videos and images that may be questionable or even shocking. Research indicates alarming trends of diminishing empathy and increasing emotional detachment among humans, with increasingly mechanistic interactions and responses.[40] While Gen Z often responded to online tragedy with activism and awareness campaigns, Gen Alpha may be more likely to encounter such content through humor or memes, potentially leading to emotional desensitization. Even if the content Gen Alpha watches is okay, not all YouTubers and Twitch streamers are good role models, which means that Gen Alpha could be partially raised by less-than-admirable characters.

The constant digital infiltration has also resulted in increased depression and mental health issues, even in young children. In 2024, US Surgeon General Vivek Murthy recommended placing warning labels on social media sites because of the immense effects of exposure to the digital world.[41]

An additional consequence of the contemporary technological landscape is the impact on children's physical development and health. Increased engagement in digital socialization at the expense of outdoor physical activity, which is crucial for developing stamina and muscle strength, has become a significant concern. Children now spend 50 percent less time playing outside in unstructured activities compared to children growing up in the 1970s. Generation Alpha children and teenagers spend on average 12.6 minutes a day in vigorous activity and more than 10 hours almost motionless.[42] Early playful movements, such as reaching and grasping, contribute to fundamental motor abilities. However, young children who are part of the "unintentional global experiment" are engrossed in their screens from the time they can hold an object. The act of holding an iPad cannot replace the necessary skills of developing hand strength and overall physical resiliency.[43] Older generations are also worried that Gen Alpha will not be proficient at practical, hands-on "hard" skills that are necessary to live.[44]

As one can imagine, social development is also hindered by excessive screen time and reduced face-to-face interactions compared to the past. Children know that they have the capability to become a quick "expert" on any topic with a few taps on their smart device. As a result, they may come across as disrespectful, as the ability to look up information online makes them bolder and more confident to fact-check what adults tell them.[45] Furthermore, in-person communication can be challenging for children or teenagers who have not developed social skills in the same way as previous generations. Although Generation Alpha is said to prefer in-person communication and collaboration more than Gen Z, they may still struggle with basic social skills.[46]

While not all members of Generation Alpha exhibit issues with these traits, some experts have observed initial trends that warrant attention. Instead of complaining about these attitudes and sometimes-questionable behavior, adult figures may want to step in as a member of the "village" that it takes to raise a child and show Gen Alpha children and teens positive behavior and habits. Social researcher Mark McCrindle encourages parents, mentors, and teachers to introduce and promote skills that will benefit Gen Alpha beyond the realm of technology.[47] One trait to develop is skepticism. Any news headline or information can be falsified on the internet. Now more than ever, it's crucial to stay alert and approach everything with a logical mindset.

Other characteristics that Gen Alpha needs to adopt are empathy, balance, resilience, and respect.[48] An article about Generation Alpha states that we need to teach these kids how to be assertive without being a bully.[49] We should also train Gen Alpha to keep an open ear and to see things from the perspectives of other people. McCrindle says, "It is the role of parents and leaders to ensure children understand technology and see the productivity benefits, but they will also need to be able to function in the world outside of technology."[50]

In a Nutshell: Challenges of Gen Alpha

- **Reduced Parental Involvement:** Many children experience less hands-on parenting due to dual-income households.
- **Premature Exposure to Adult Content:** Technology exposes children to inappropriate or conflicting content at a young age.

- **Commercial Targeting of Tweens:** Children aged eight to twelve are heavily marketed to, accelerating their psychological development and shortening their childhoods.
- **Dehumanization Through Screens:** Limited real-world interaction can lead to emotional detachment and mechanistic social behavior.
- **Poor Role Models:** Influencers and streamers may not always model positive behavior, affecting children's development in a less-than-desirable way.
- **Mental Health Concerns:** Increased screen time correlates with rising rates of depression and mental health issues in children.
- **Physical Health Decline:** Less outdoor play and physical activity lead to weaker motor skills and reduced physical resilience.
- **Lack of Practical Skills:** Gen Alpha may not develop essential hands-on or "hard" life skills.
- **Social Skill Deficits:** Reduced face-to-face interaction may hinder development of basic social and communication skills.
- **Overconfidence in Technology:** Easy access to information can make children overly confident and potentially disrespectful toward adults.
- **Need for Character Development:** Traits like empathy, resilience, skepticism, and respect need to be actively taught and nurtured.

Strengths

Generation Alpha retains a potent amount of digital intelligence. Digital intelligence enables individuals to communicate effectively through technology and to comprehend and mitigate digital safety. It includes digital literacy, the ability to effectively evaluate, synthesize, and share information found online.[51] Generation Alpha leverages its digital literacy to stay continuously connected with the global community. Events happening globally can be quickly known and become more impactful due to social media and the internet. Being consistently online can be advantageous, as it keeps individuals informed about global events and aware of happenings beyond their local area. Generation Alpha is consequently more in tune with the bigger picture than one might expect for their age.

Greater hand-eye coordination and visual skills are also benefits of increased time with technology due to the digital games they often play, which require finesse and refined abilities to complete sophisticated tasks. Generation Alpha also exhibits heightened perceptual abilities and more advanced skills in rhythmically interpreting music and effectively using numbers.[52]

Like their Gen Z predecessors, Gen Alpha kids also hold equality among races, ages, and genders as important, and they see the value of preserving the earth through environmentally conscious practices. Part of this is due to parental influence, and part is due to messages shared on social media and other platforms with which Gen Alpha may interact.

Another positive trait of Gen Alpha is the potential for heightened active learning and participation. Gen Alpha consists of logical, strategic, and creative thinkers and learners. Nihal Yurtseven and Şirin Karadeniz state, "Alpha children acquire knowledge much better by active participation in the learning process through experiments, cooperative learning, problem-solving activities or drama."[53]

In conclusion, Generation Alpha stands at the forefront of a rapidly evolving digital era characterized by unprecedented access to technology and information. While they face unique challenges, such as reduced social interaction and increased screen time, they also possess remarkable strengths in digital literacy, creativity, and adaptability. As they navigate a world shaped by technological advancements and shifting family dynamics, it is crucial for parents, educators, and mentors to provide the guidance and support needed to foster their development into well-rounded, empathetic, and resilient individuals. By understanding and addressing the distinctive needs and potential of Generation Alpha, we can help them harness their capabilities to create a positive and impactful future.

In a Nutshell: Strengths of Gen Alpha

- **High Digital Intelligence:** Skilled in using technology for communication and problem-solving, they possess a strong understanding of digital safety and responsible online behavior.
- **Proficient in Digital Literacy:** They readily evaluate, synthesize, and share online information.
- **Global Awareness:** Constant connectivity keeps them informed about global events, and they are more attuned to worldwide issues and perspectives from a young age.

- **Enhanced Cognitive and Motor Skills:** Digital gaming has resulted in improved hand-eye coordination and visual processing and advanced perceptual abilities, musical rhythm interpretation, and numerical skills.
- **Social and Environmental Values:** Influenced by both parents and digital media, they hold a strong belief in equality across races, ages, and genders and are environmentally conscious.
- **Active and Strategic Learners:** They thrive in hands-on, participatory learning environments and excel in logical, strategic, and creative thinking. They prefer learning through experiments, problem-solving, and collaboration.
- **Adaptability and Creativity:** They are comfortable navigating rapid technological changes and capable of creative expression and innovation in digital spaces.
- **Potential for Empathy and Balance:** With proper guidance, they can develop empathy, resilience, and respect. They are open to learning how to balance assertiveness with kindness and confidence with humility.

Notes

1   "Word of the Year: 'App,'" CBS News, January 8, 2011, https://www.cbsnews.com/news/word-of-the-year-app/.
2   Mark McCrindle and Ashley Fell, *Understanding Generation Alpha* (McCrindle, 2020), https://generationalpha.com/wp-content/uploads/2020/02/Understanding-Generation-Alpha-McCrindle.pdf.
3   Mark McCrindle, "Busting Myths About Generation Alpha," McCrindle, 2021, https://mccrindle.com.au/article/topic/generation-alpha/busting-myths-about-generation-alpha/.
4   U.S. Census Bureau, *Exploring Age Groups in the 2020 Census*, interactive visualization, accessed November 13, 2025, https://www.census.gov/library/visualizations/interactive/exploring-age-groups-in-the-2020-census.html.
5   Çiğdem Apaydin and Feyza Kaya, "An Analysis of the Preschool Teachers' Views on Alpha Generation," *European Journal of Education Studies* 6, no. 11 (2020): 125, https://doi.org/10.5281/zenodo.3627158.
6   Alena Höfrová, Venera Balidemaj, and Mark A. Small, "A Systematic Literature Review of Education for Generation Alpha," *Discover Education* 3, no. 125 (2024): 3, https://doi.org/10.1007/s44217-024-00218-3.

7. Harsh Kundra, "Coding, a Core Skill for Generation Alpha," *Times of India*, September 23, 2022, https://timesofindia.indiatimes.com/blogs/voices/coding-a-core-skill-for-generation-alpha/.
8. "Educators and Generation Alpha: Adapting to the Future of Learning," Holistique Training, October 2, 2024, https://holistiquetraining.com/public/en/news/education.
9. Höfrová, Balidemaj, and Small, "Systematic Literature Review," 2.
10. Dom Barnard, "History of VR—Timeline of Events and Tech Development," *VirtualSpeech* (blog), October 17, 2024, https://virtualspeech.com/blog/history-of-vr.
11. "Coding Robots," Makeblock, accessed October 10, 2025, https://www.makeblock.com/collections/coding-robots.
12. "Cozmo Robot 2.0: Features Setup and Where to Buy in 2025," Anki Cozmo Robot, accessed October 10, 2025, https://ankicozmorobot.com/.
13. "Coding Toys," Learning Resources, accessed October 10, 2025, https://www.learningresources.com/shop/category/coding.
14. McCrindle and Fell, *Understanding Generation Alpha*.
15. Erika Marzano, "Relatable, Real, Raw: TikTok's Power in News for Gen Z," Fix, November 1, 2024, https://thefix.media/2024/11/1/relatable-real-raw-tiktoks-power-in-news-for-gen-z.
16. Eugene Charniak, *AI and I: An Intellectual History of Artificial Intelligence* (MIT Press, 2024), 93–111.
17. Chuck Brooks, *Inside Cyber: How AI, 5G, IoT, and Quantum Computing Will Transform Privacy and Our Security* (John Wiley & Sons, 2025), 59.
18. "How Roblox Became the New Social Media for Gen Z and Alpha," Exclusible, updated May 9, 2024, https://www.exclusible.com/resources/how-roblox-became-the-new-social-media-for-gen-z-and-alpha/.
19. Ibid.
20. Nihal Yurtseven and Şirin Karadeniz, "An Overview of Generation Alpha," in *The Teacher of Generation Alpha*, ed. Nihal Yurtseven, 11–32 (Peter Lang, 2020), 13.
21. Klaus Zierer, *Educating the Covid Generation: How We Can Prevent the Impending Educational Catastrophe After Covid* (Routledge, 2025), 2, https://doi.org/10.4324/9781003408864.
22. Michael Spurlin, "Meet Generation Alpha: Who Are They, and How Do We Educate Them?" *ATPE News*, Summer 2024, https://atpe.org/News-Media/Magazine/ATPE-News-Summer-2024/Generation-Alpha.
23. Yurtseven and Karadeniz, "Overview of Generation Alpha," 12–13.
24. "New Report on Generation Alpha—Characteristics of the Youngest Generation," on Henry Rose Lee's official website, 2020, https://www.intergenerationalexpert.com/new-report-generation-alpha-characteristics-youngest/.
25. Daisy Thomas, "The Future Is Alpha," Medium, June 19, 2024, https://medium.com/@daisygarciathomas/the-future-is-alpha-8f9d3e75efe3.
26. Helenor Gilmour, "Raising Gen Alpha: How Millennial Parenting Is Impacting the Next Generation," Research World, May 4, 2023, https://researchworld.com/articles/raising-gen-alpha-how-millennial-parenting-is-impacting-the-next-generation.

27 Pumudu A. Fernando and H. K. Salinda Premadasa, "Use of Gamification and Game-Based Learning in Educating Generation Alpha: A Systematic Literature Review," *Educational Technology and Society* 27, no. 2 (April 2024): 114–32, https://doi.org/10.30191/ETS.202404_27(2).RP03.
28 Andry Chowanda, Yen Lina Prasetio, Nicodemus, and Naufal Rizdki Fadhlurrahman, "Designing Digital Games as Learning Tools for Mathematics," *ICIC Express Letters* 14, no. 9 (September 2020): 927–34, https://doi.org/10.24507/icicel.14.09.927.
29 Yurtseven and Karadeniz, "Overview of Generation Alpha," 16.
30 McCrindle and Fell, *Understanding Generation Alpha*.
31 Jessica Kato, "What Educators Need to Know About Generation Alpha," EdSurge, February 2, 2024, https://www.edsurge.com/news/2024-02-02-what-educators-need-to-know-about-generation-alpha.
32 Ibid.
33 Yurtseven and Karadeniz, "Overview of Generation Alpha," 16.
34 "Part 2: Understanding Generation Z vs. Generation Alpha," Destination Knowledge, October 23, 2024, https://destinationknowledge.com/part-2-understanding-generation-z-vs-gen-alpha/#:~:text=Curiosity%20and%20Personalization%3A%20Valuing%20individuality,highly%20effective%20for%20this%20generation.
35 Höfrová, Balidemaj, and Small, "Systematic Literature Review," 14–15.
36 Fernando Filgueiras, "Artificial Intelligence and Education Governance," *Education, Citizenship and Social Justice* 19, no. 3 (November 2024): 349–61, https://doi.org/10.1177/17461979231160674.
37 "The Impact of Social Media and Technology on Gen Alpha," *Annie E. Casey Foundation*, (blog), June 22, 2025, https://www.aecf.org/blog/impact-of-social-media-on-gen-alpha.
38 McCrindle and Fell, *Understanding Generation Alpha*.
39 Edgar Demeter, Dana Rad, and Evelina Balaș, "Schadenfreude and General Anti-Social Behaviours: The Role of Violent Content Preferences and Life Satisfaction," *BRAIN: Broad Research in Artificial Intelligence and Neuroscience* 12, no. 2 (June 2021): 99–100, https://brain.edusoft.ro/index.php/brain/article/view/1142.
40 Izabela Marszałek-Kotzur, "Cognitive Technologies—Are We in Danger of Humanizing Machines and Dehumanizing Humans?" *Management Systems in Production Engineering* 30, no. 3 (September 2022): 269–75, https://doi.org/10.2478/mspe-2022-0034.
41 Ibid.
42 Bryana Hinck, "Missing: Childhood's Playtime," Thrive Pediatrics, May 29, 2024, https://thrive-pediatrics.com/2024/05/29/missing-childhoods-playtime/.
43 Jeffrey Trawick-Smith, *The Physical Play and Motor Development of Young Children: A Review of Literature and Implications for Practice* (Center for Early Childhood Education, n.d.).
44 McCrindle and Fell, *Understanding Generation Alpha*.
45 Lauren Brown West-Rosenthal, "Gen Alpha Isn't a Uniquely Disrespectful Generation—They're Just Misunderstood," *Parents*, updated January 10, 2025, https://www.parents.com/gen-alpha-kids-disrespectful-or-misunderstood-8725182.

46 "New Report on Generation Alpha."
47 Mark McCrindle, "Raising Gen Alpha in the Great Screen Age," McCrindle, 2022, https://mccrindle.com.au/article/raising-gen-alpha-in-the-great-screen-age/.
48 Ibid.
49 Taylor Knight, "Is Gen Alpha Disrespectful or Just Misunderstood? Why Confident Kids Are 'Confronting Authority' with a 'Strong Voice,'" *New York Post*, August 29, 2024, https://nypost.com/2024/08/29/lifestyle/is-gen-alpha-disrespectful-or-just-misunderstood-why-confident-kids-are-confronting-authority-with-a-strong-voice/.
50 McCrindle, "Raising Gen Alpha."
51 Hülya Avcı and Tufan Adıgüzel, "Leveraging Digital Intelligence in Generation Alpha," in *The Teacher of Generation Alpha*, ed. Nihal Yurtseven, 119–32 (Peter Lang, 2020), 119–32, https://doi.org/10.3726/b16823.
52 Apaydin and Kaya, "Analysis of Preschool Teachers' Views."
53 Yurtseven and Karadeniz, "Overview of Generation Alpha," 16.

5 Striking the Right Chord
Addressing Generations Z and Alpha Challenges and Strengths in Piano Teaching

Challenges of Gen Z Piano Students

Every generation of students has their own distinctive traits, some that enhance their educational experience and others that introduce challenges. The learning hurdles that Generation Z students face may be different from those of a student of previous years, but they are no less capable than students of the past. The environment and events that Generation Z has experienced have shaped them and in turn equipped them with some great strengths. On that same note, Gen Z's upbringing has also passed along some other characteristics that are useful for teachers to be aware of as they teach and eventually work alongside these younger musicians.

From Card Catalogs to Chatbots

Imagine for a minute that you are writing a five-hundred-word paper on giraffes for a school assignment. You need to find out their mating habits, diet, social patterns, and classifications. Now picture this assignment in 1985. What do you do for this research project? Where do you start? Likely, you would start by walking down to your local library and asking the librarian where books on animals are located. Then, you would either spend some time taking notes in the library, or you would check out a book to bring home for your research. You also probably checked out a book on how to write a proper bibliography, just in case. Then, you would take what you have learned and write out your assignment by hand in legible, neat handwriting or type it out on a word processor. You also take out your MLA manual and painstakingly write out your references. This process took up a good part of your afternoon and evening, but you had the satisfaction of finishing your work. Then, you would need to remember to bring the physical paper to school the next day and return any library books you checked out.

Flash forward ten years to 1995, and this assignment has probably become a bit faster. The school may have a computer with educational software, or if you are lucky, you have access to the World Wide Web and can research your project on AltaVista or the World Wide Web Virtual Library. Typing out a bibliography is still a pain, but you can quickly backspace and fix mistakes and format hanging indents. Additionally, you may have been able to type out your assignment on a word-processing software installed on your computer and print it directly from your device that is hardwired to a printer. The printer is slow, but it beats writing out your assignment by hand!

In 2005, many families have a computer in their home, and schools have entire computer labs, so this paper is even easier now. This assignment can be completed by accessing Google or the hundreds of educational sites and readily available software. As someone who is familiar with PCs, you type out your search terms in your program or website of choice, design your document with a fun font in Microsoft Word, and even include some images. For the bibliography, you go to the new website Citation Machine and fill in the information of your sources, and voilà—there are your references! After you are satisfied with your work, you print out your paper in color and double-sided.

If you are tired of researching giraffes, don't worry—we are going to complete this assignment one final time but now in the present day. It is 12:00 p.m., and you want to get this paper out of the way so you can enjoy your lunch. You type your paper instructions into your favorite AI chatbot, ChatGPT, and ask it to make an outline for you. You also ask for some reliable sources, and ChatGPT gives you a list to check out. You skim these articles and e-books and then type out your paragraphs based on the outline ChatGPT gave you, including pictures that it shared with you. You are confident in your work, but you ask ChatGPT to check your grammar and reword a few sentences for you. Then, you ask ChatGPT to write your bibliography, and within seconds you have your references. You double-check a YouTube short to make sure it is correct. It is now 12:25, and you submit your assignment online. By 2:00 p.m., you barely remember completing that assignment on whatever that topic was. You have a show playing on your laptop, have played a game on your phone, have watched Instagram Reels, and have texted five friends about totally different things while FaceTiming another friend. Life moves fast, and you cannot hamper your schedule with things that take too much time.

Quick Wins: The Appeal and Impact of Instant Gratification

The point of this time-travel activity was to illustrate how and why Generation Z expects instant results. Students tend to carry the "quick action/quick response" from the digital world to the piano studio.[1] Sitting down and practicing a single piece for thirty minutes a day with an end goal of completing it in three months is almost impossible for an inexperienced musician's mind to comprehend today. Additionally, if a student struggles with a passage, then they may become frustrated and not know how to proceed. Worse yet, the student may disregard the piece and perhaps the concept of practice altogether because they do not see the results within moments of the first attempt. While this seems drastic, this is reality, and though it may not happen overnight, a student may separate from the piano because it feels like a lost cause or an unattainable project.

A teacher working with Generation Z students experiencing these feelings should assist them in setting achievable, smaller goals and provide support, especially at the start of this process. Students also need to realize the value of consistent, focused work. One way an instructor can promote a healthy work ethic in piano study is to ask for check-in videos or audio of a student practicing. This can allow the student to have "supervision" in their practice sessions, which provides an incentive to stay locked into what they are playing. A teacher may also choose to draw out a progress map, either for general playing or a specific piece, as shown in figure 5.1.

Progress maps are especially useful to postmillennial students for two reasons: gamification and visual learning. Gamification is the "use of game elements in non-game environments."[2] Due to the countless apps and games that twenty-first-century students often play in their downtime, they are very receptive to games in any context. A progress map shows "levels" that a student will need to "pass" in order to accomplish the end goal. Another reason progress maps appeal to Gen Z students is the visual aspect. Gen Z and Gen Alpha are highly responsive to learning through visual stimuli, such as images and videos; learning from plain text seems to be less effective.[3] Students will appreciate if some color and creativity is added to the progress map and will likely respond positively and remember these levels of progression more vividly.

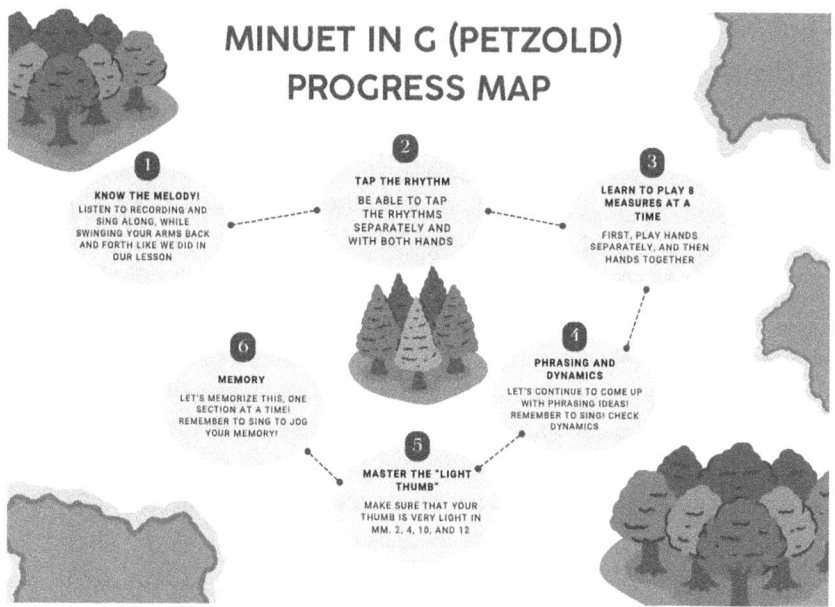

Figure 5.1 Sample progress map for Christian Petzold's Minuet in G. *Illustration by the author.*

To further combat the ever-present feeling of immediacy students are surrounded with, teachers can be intentional about celebrating small wins and showering students with much positive affirmation when they are showing small signs of understanding the task at hand and displaying good practice techniques. Start with praise for small accomplishments, then increase the standard as the student progresses through their musical journey.

Now That's ~~Entertainment~~ Education!

Gen Z is infiltrated with hours of content each day, with flashing lights and colors and information and humor coming to them by the truckload. Students of today respond most positively to visual and experiential learning.[4] Rothman states, "Because their [members of Gen Z] use of technology has developed the visual ability portion of their brains, visual forms of learning are more effective for these learners."[5] Additionally, a report by the National Eye Institute states that visual processing is "shaped by our experiences" and the activity of neurons in the brain can adapt and will become more adept at certain tasks at the expense of other tasks.[6] Because students are in a world much more reliant on visual stimuli and technology, the way they take in information is different from before. Gen Z is quicker at understanding concepts in a visually stimulating manner but perhaps slower when merely hearing instructions or reading plain text. Education is seeing a shift from traditional lectures to more hands-on, digital-based learning.[7]

How can piano teachers incorporate more visual and digital modes of learning in piano lessons? One idea is to record videos of yourself playing a certain technical concept that you teach to your students and add them to an unlisted (or public, if you want to reach beyond your studio) YouTube playlist. This way, you can quickly pull from your repository of demonstration videos and share with your students at the appropriate times in their piano studies. Then students can watch the video outside of lessons and will likely remember the content in a much more meaningful way. On the same note, useful videos for many different areas, such as music history, music theory, rhythm exercises, and more, can be added to a playlist to share with students as supplemental material during the week or even briefly during the lesson. Learning from a YouTube video will feel natural to the typical Gen Z student, as studies show that this generation visits this site daily for both entertainment and educational purposes.[8]

Another way a teacher can adopt digital tools is to use such apps as Tenuto for drilling music theory and ear-training concepts. Tenuto combines factors of visual stimuli, digital integration, and gamification in one activity while improving the student's grasp on these important concepts. There are many other worthwhile mobile applications that a teacher can use in the studio, like Note Rush, which functions as a digital note-reading drill; Piano Maestro, which is a fun and interactive sight-reading activity; and Rhythm Swing, which gamifies completing rhythm exercises. A bimonthly quick search of the App Store or Google Play Store can help to keep teachers on track with the latest apps.

Technology-based feedback can benefit Gen Z education, as well. Teens and young adults often communicate digitally, including texting, Facebook Messenger, WhatsApp, Instagram, TikTok, and other platforms. Since the first text message in 1992 that read, "Merry Christmas," electronic messaging as a means of silent, instantaneous conversation has evolved and exponentially grown.[9] From 363 billion text messages in 2007 to 6 billion texts *per day* in 2021 (an increase of approximately 500 percent), just texting has exploded, without even considering other messaging platforms.[10] Because this is such a natural method of correspondence, teachers may feel comfortable texting students directly, or in a group chat with a parent if a student is under eighteen, and sharing resources, practice progress, and other valuable information. It is easy to share YouTube video links, Google Docs, articles, and anything else digital (which comprises most of what we experience today)!

The Multitasking Mindset

Gen Zers will likely have a difficult time trying to focus on one task at a time. Often, young people put on a show on TV while scrolling through Reels on their smartphones while messaging a friend from their computers. There is even an ongoing joke that younger audiences cannot process information without looking at something else at the same time, such as *Subway Surfers* or ASMR videos.[11] While it appears that young people are just better at multitasking and perhaps their brains can handle multiple sources of information at once, the reality is our brains are not meant to capture so many elements simultaneously. Multitasking can at times be useful for menial tasks or for navigating through sophisticated tasks that require many parts, but it often impairs the accuracy of metacognitive monitoring, emphasizing the need for focused attention on primary tasks to improve learning and performance.

Teachers can design tasks that incorporate various elements and methods, creating the illusion of multiple activities when it is actually a single task. For instance, a student might be assigned to practice the exposition of a Beethoven sonata. The teacher can guide the student to focus on several aspects while playing, such as articulation, tempo consistency, dynamics, the balancing of voices, phrasing, and other crucial factors. Additionally, the teacher can use drum-set backing tracks to enhance the perception of complexity, making it seem like more is happening than there truly is.

Support Systems: Enhancing Student Success

Students and people in general have always needed support and guidance. However, today's piano students require distinct support, as Gen Z faces unique challenges. One barrier is being overwhelmed with longer-term goals and practicing. In a 2021 study on Generation Z piano students, teachers identified several factors contributing to their students' feelings of being overwhelmed, including a loss of motivation when tasks are not completed quickly, a preference for the digital world, high levels of professional anxiety, undeveloped social functioning, and poor stress-management skills.[12]

A possible solution to the problem is to create personalized learning experiences through self-discovery of learning preferences, personality type, and previous study. Another idea is to provide detailed instructions for assignments, as members of Gen Z sometimes need a little help on how to effectively complete tasks with the never-ending storm of distractions around them. An educational study on Gen Z students states, "Assignments that require students to access information online should be very clear as to goals, sources, time-spent, ways to glean and evaluate the content."[13]

In a world brimming with distractions, self-reflection has become more essential than ever, enabling students to understand their own functioning and reactions to stress and external events. Familiarity with oneself and self-reflection also can counter the tendency of Gen Z to react more temperamentally, as they often mix work and emotions. Gen Z tends to be in touch with their emotions, which is a positive characteristic, however their mentors can encourage them to explore their emotions alongside mature methods of handling them. In other words, Gen Z can use guidance on emotional intelligence. According to an article, zoomers (another term this group has been called) have experienced a decline in key emotional and cognitive skills, including identifying and understanding their emotions, recognizing recurring thought or behavior patterns, evaluating decisions thoughtfully, managing their feelings, staying motivated by meaningful values, and envisioning new possibilities.[14]

To combat high anxiety levels, teachers can facilitate conversations with students about burnout, self-care, and mindfulness techniques. Self-care isn't just about taking time off to recover from work (though it can include that); it often also involves maintaining an organized schedule and clean environments and making healthy dietary and lifestyle choices.

Strengths of Gen Z Piano Students

Architects of Their Own Learning Landscapes

Gen Z students have been described as curious, determined, open-minded, and independent.[15] Students today ask more questions than students did before, and they want to know how a particular skill will benefit them in the future. Gen Zers are also eager to start working—they have drive—but they need a little extra guidance on how to achieve their goals, and as a result, they are often misunderstood as unmotivated or lazy.[16] This generation is driven not only to learn but also to create positive change in the world, aspiring to be at the forefront of movements that aim to achieve it.[17]

Gen Z students are open-minded and eager to learn about other cultures, helping to shed light on underrepresented and underperformed composers and cultures. Online communication has expanded Gen Z's social circle, making it easier for individuals with similar interests to connect, even if they are from different parts of the globe.[18] Thanks to their extensive immersion in global cultures via social media, which connects countries within seconds, Gen Z is always ready to learn and collaborate with their peers around the world. This characteristic is highly positive and opens the floodgates for teachers to educate their students on world music, history, new music, and underperformed composers.

Independence is a trait that many Gen Z students were forced to pick up during the COVID-19 pandemic. Across the globe, classes from kindergarten to graduate schools were abruptly shifted to fully online, often in a matter of hours. Students had to sit through hours of online lectures and often missed core concepts due to the nature of the abrupt online course structures. In a 2020 report on education during the pandemic, NewsRX stated that most teachers continued to use a "teacher-centered" format, characterized by an abundance of lectures and difficult-to-access information. Consequently, many instructors were unable to fully use online tools, leaving many students feeling frustrated and lost. Instead, students took advantage of such tools as YouTube to supplement their education, and at times this was even encouraged.[19] Despite the chaos that both students and teachers faced during the pandemic and the inevitable negative impacts on young people, students emerged with the valuable skill of independent learning, thanks to their resilience.

In the context of piano lessons, teachers can take advantage of these characteristics and enrich their musical education. When it comes to studying the context of a piece, for example, a teacher can give some general guidance on where to start looking, and a student will likely take this assignment and run with it. Students today often like going down a rabbit hole, as they often call their mini research sessions, and emerge from their explorations with many useful findings. Students know where to look: YouTube, articles, and even creators on TikTok and Instagram post educational content from which Gen Z enjoys learning. If the content is about a lesser-known, niche topic or subject matter that pertains to global music, a student will likely be extra motivated to learn.

Wired for Success: Gen Z's Technological Edge

Generation Z is what some researchers refer to as "digital natives" or "digital integrators," depending on the year they were born. Either way, technology for Gen Z is "almost like the air they breathe, permeating all areas of their lifestyle and relationships."[20] Karina Ochis, in her book about Gen Z in the workplace, says, "Technology is not merely a tool for this group, but a fundamental aspect of their approach—instinctive, ever-present, and essential."[21] Even the most senior member of Generation Z (born 1995) is well versed in technology through mobile devices and social media, as well as any new digital tools that appear on the horizon. Gen Z is familiar with texting, video calls, group chats, instant/disappearing messages, and any other available form of communication. Interestingly, however, despite the plethora of digital communication at Gen Z's fingertips, their preferred method of communication is face-to-face.[22]

Social media holds great importance for Gen Z, whose members are adept at using various platforms for distinct purposes, optimizing each platform's features for specific tasks. Snapchat is used for more private conversations and a more intimate audience.[23] It is not uncommon for Gen Z to create a secondary Instagram account, called a Finsta, to share more personal and authentic pictures and updates with a smaller group of friends.[24] And if you know a member of Gen Z, you could likely testify that one would be hard pressed to find a typical Gen Zer who holds an active Facebook account, as this platform is considered outdated. Ironically, Facebook was created for college students, but times have changed, and the future of social media is moving away from text and into photos and videos.[25]

Me, Myself, and AI

On November 30, 2022, OpenAI made its public debut of its chatbot ChatGPT. This event captivated the interest of billions of people, and one cannot talk about technology without mentioning artificial intelligence (AI). From its 1960s experimental origins to machine learning and automated chess players, AI has transformed tech companies and, by the 2020s, affects nearly every profession, education sector, and individual.[26] AI has allowed for tools that help with coding, presentation preparation, grammar checking, stock predictions, trip planning, song lyric writing, and much more—so much more that this paragraph could easily spill over into an entire book of its own.

Gen Z is so proficient at technology, so how does AI affect them? Reports have shown that Gen Z display effective usage of AI tools in the workplace and education. Gen Z is adept at working smarter, not harder, in many instances. Shubham Agarwal, in her *Business Insider* article about Gen Z's workplace savviness, describes a twenty-one-year-old corporate employee who used OtterAI to transcribe meetings and conversations within seconds—an excellent example of how Gen Z is using tools available to them to increase productivity and reduce menial tasks.[27]

Of course, as with anything in this world, the pros are accompanied by cons, and the option for misuse is ever present. AI can deliver inaccurate information because it creates answers based on previous data.[28] However, Gen Z is realistic and recognizes the downfalls of AI. In a conversation I had with Gen Z university students in a class about music and society, the students were almost in total agreement that AI poses concerns and potentially detrimental effects to humans. Students were aware that AI gives inaccurate information, and many were vocal about the fact that they did not want AI to "do the work for them" when it came to learning. The students also expressed that they felt badly for the next generation (Gen Alpha), who would not know a world before AI and would likely have a more difficult time distinguishing between AI-generated content and content created by people.

In a summary like those you might find by AI on a Google search (except this one, which is written by a human!), one could surmise that Gen Z is smart, sharp, and savvy. Gen Z readily uses AI for time-consuming, routine tasks while recognizing when a personal touch is necessary. They understand that educational content created by AI is not necessarily accurate, and they are motivated to dig deeper to find the source when they are looking for a true answer to a question.

In a broader technological sense, Gen Z is comfortable using mobile applications for learning and communicating, partly because they were born into a world of tech and partly because of the pandemic. Any digitally based assignment a teacher gives a Gen Z student will more likely be positively received. There will be little to no learning curve, and on top of that, there is a good chance that the student will enjoy the format of learning something on a screen, as Gen Z lives and breathes technology.[29] Incorporating technology is a good idea, as there are many benefits to using such tools as digital note and rhythm drills, interactive sight-reading games, YouTube demonstration videos, and audio- and video-recording apps. We have these great tools available to us, so why not use them?

The Unique Perspective of Generation Alpha

Generation Alpha is the first generation to be fully born in the twenty-first century, and because of their exposure to screens since birth, they are called the world's "unintentional experiment."[30] While this sounds rather ominous, there is much to look forward to with this new group of students. Remember, there is a gap between the generations regarding phrases and terms that are now obsolete among younger people. Because technology is advancing so quickly, there is likely a shock when one hears what Gen Alpha is not familiar with in the 2020s. Brace yourself for this list of items and activities that today's children and even teens may not know:

- **Landline Telephones:** A typical member of Gen Alpha may not have even seen a landline phone before.
- **Dial-Up Internet:** This is a relic of the past and likely an unknown historical factoid.
- **VHS Tapes:** Gen Alpha kids may not recognize a VHS tape, as Netflix and other streaming services became commonplace before they were born.
- **CDs and DVDs:** While DVDs may seem like a more modern invention, they are considered old tech now for the same reason as VHS tapes: streaming services.
- **Printed Encyclopedias:** A Generation Alpha student might be unfamiliar with encyclopedias and may not realize that Wikipedia serves as the modern, digital equivalent of what was once commonplace.
- **Nondigital Toys:** Many Gen Alpha kids do not see the appeal of action figures, building blocks, and board games.
- **Outdoor Games:** Gen Alpha does not venture outside as much and instead stays indoors playing on their devices.
- **Radio:** Radio broadcasting may seem like another relic of the past.

- **Letters and Postcards:** Handwriting is less common, and so are handwritten letters. A Gen Alpha would probably tell you, "Why write a letter and wait days when you can text a message and send it immediately?"
- **Brick-and-Mortar Stores:** Since Amazon's and other online stores' takeovers of the shopping scene, it is uncommon for Gen Alpha to look at items, such as toys, in a physical store.
- **Maps:** Acquainting yourself with the area using a map? Why not just use Apple or Google Maps, which give you step-by-step directions?
- **Film Cameras:** The days of taking film to be developed are gone unless you are trying to be "retro" by using a film camera "for the vibes."
- **Physical Libraries:** A member of Generation Alpha may have never set foot in a library unless it was an online one.

This list highlights just a few examples of the changes that have occurred over the past ten to twenty years. Generation Alpha is truly living in the future, swiftly embracing modern versions of past items to enhance efficiency and convenience. These significant differences in their upbringing compared to previous generations do not suggest that today's children are less intelligent or ignorant. Rather, they highlight the fact that childhood has evolved dramatically, necessitating adaptations in teaching methods.

Keep Up!

Today's teachers are surrounded by a plethora of new technological possibilities and may feel overwhelmed by the sea of digital innovations. While effective educators strive to incorporate modern tools into their teaching, it is impossible to learn and use every invention. Additionally, a vast amount of the world's knowledge is available at students' fingertips. Kids today are exposed to an unlimited number of teaching videos and styles, making them rich in educational resources. Because they are so familiar with various teaching environments and styles, students can easily detect a lack of originality or effort. If Generation Alpha children see someone using a widely adopted trend or method, they might label it as "cringe." Teachers of Gen Alpha are encouraged to think outside the box, try unconventional methods, and always strive for innovative and original thinking.[31] Instead of trying to keep up with every digital addition to your teaching, focus on using your creative side to keep your teaching fresh.

Challenges of Gen Alpha Piano Students

Emotional Intelligence

Gen Alpha kids are experts at using applications that move quickly, which results in quick thinking and fast problem-solving. However, young brains nowadays do not have the time to sit on things that cannot be rushed, such as processing feelings, thoughts, and emotions. There is not a quick fix or an app that can do this for a person. Parents once commonly taught such skills as managing emotional reactions to challenges and weighing the pros and cons of decisions. However, in today's family, both parents are often working, and everyone is juggling a hectic schedule. In the limited downtime that a mother and father may have with their children, the common go-to activity is the TV or other forms of screen time. It is easier and allows one to dissociate from the world's problems and today's faster pace. However, adults should create environments that allow for both digital and social-emotional learning.

In addition to Gen Alpha's chaotic lifestyle and lack of supervision, they are being "'raised' on the open internet," as one Reddit user put it.[32] Especially during COVID-19, parents were not able to monitor screen time like before, and kids ingested all sorts of content without many (or any) limits.[33] Online video content can overwhelm the mind with material that encourages mocking people of all ages and laughing at accidents and repetitive, trivial content in short videos (such as Reels and TikToks), often referred to as "brain rot."[34] As a result of today's society, environment, and family dynamics, impulse control, empathy, and emotional awareness are lacking in Generation Alpha.[35] Adding to the challenges of prolonged screen time, the pandemic appears to have triggered developmental delays and learning loss in some Generation Alpha students, who spent crucial formative years with minimal outside interaction.[36]

Because members of Generation Alpha are also encouraged (either in person or online) to question convention and to self-express, they can communicate with apparent attitude deficiencies. In other words, many Gen Alphas won't just take your word for it if you tell them something. They may fact-check you or be skeptical. If older generations had access to so much knowledge at their fingertips when they were younger, wouldn't they be tempted to also double-check any facts shared with them? After all, almost everyone can recall a time when someone relayed faulty information to them! So making sure that information is correct and knowing how to access reliable sources is not bad in and of itself. However, Gen Alpha needs to be taught to properly convey what they are thinking and to remain curious but in a way that is respectful of authority.

It has been said that it takes a village to raise a child, and this is still true! A recent and sad observation is that there seems to be no village for Generation Alpha.[37] Parents' schedules are overloaded, and many children are placed in front of a screen as a digital babysitter and virtual playground.[38] Educators and anyone who plays a mentorship role for a Gen Alpha child or teen has the capacity to positively influence their life. Generation Alpha has many admirable qualities and potential for greatness. However, as a news article title puts it, "Gen Alpha Kids Know More than Us but Need Guidance" because their intelligence and curiosity can bring them down.[39] Psychologist Catherine Nobile, in an article written by Lauren Brown West-Rosenthal, states, "The secret is to help Gen Alpha develop the balance between assertiveness and being assertive, between being strong and being tough, between confidence and being a bully, and between self-esteem and arrogance."[40]

Now, a piano instructor's main job is to teach the art of piano to their studio members, but you as the piano teacher of a Gen Alpha student can play a bigger role than you think! Some practical assistance that teachers can give to their Gen Alpha students include the following:

- **Model respectful communication.** Illustrate with an easy-to-read, attractive visual in the studio.
- **Teach active listening.** Take the time to explain what this looks like in a lesson scenario.
- **Set boundaries.** Be more specific than you feel you have to. Chances are, Generation Alpha students have good intentions but may not have fully mastered some of the manners that were once considered commonplace by the time we would typically expect them to.

Distractions

Generation Alpha students have so many wonderful opportunities available to them, but perhaps the abundance of after-school activities on top of preexisting distractions is too much for them. A teacher on a piano teacher

Facebook group commented that there is a culture for parents to enroll their children in many classes and activities so they can try everything.[41] When Gen Alpha kids reach their teen years, it's already time to start thinking about steps after high school.

College admissions are becoming more competitive, and students are buffing up their résumé as early as junior high. College student Lucas Benjamin writes, "College admissions have become a high-stakes process, as students are now expected to apply with not only exceptional grades but also an impressive range of extracurriculars, leadership roles, internships, and personal essays that must stand out in a sea of thousands of other applicants."[42] Generation Alpha students are not only enrolled in numerous extracurricular activities for the enjoyment and skill-building opportunities they provide but also because participation is almost mandatory if they want to have a wide range of college options in the future.

Practice

Generation Alpha students participate in so many activities that do not require them to show up with much or any preparatory work, but they still experience burnout.[43] However, learning the piano takes consistent, diligent practice between lessons! As many piano instructors know, parental involvement, especially in the beginning, is *crucial* to a student's success. Parents are already balancing work and transporting their children to extracurricular activities, so the (often) unexpected responsibility of supervising practice sessions adds yet another task to their busy schedules.

Now, let's say that a student has parents who make sure their child practices six days a week, and this student is motivated and wants to play the piano. Unfortunately, the student may have a bit more trouble adjusting to the skill of practicing than previous generations had. An article written by a team of neuroscientists and psychologists says of Gen Alpha, "They're bouncing between apps, games, and videos faster than you can say 'focus.' It's like their brains are wired for constant stimulation, always craving the next dopamine hit from a new piece of content."[44] Functioning offline may be a struggle for a Gen Alpha kid in today's world, but gamifying practice techniques, incorporating technology when possible, and encouraging your Generation Alpha student will go a long way in their progress.

Motor Skills

If you have read any portion of the earlier chapters, you can surmise that technology is a huge theme when discussing both Gen Z and Gen Alpha. Phone and tablet usage is prevalent in Generation Alpha kids. So far, we have discussed the effects that overuse of devices can have on one's attention span, work ethic, and even attitude. However, the physical implications of digital overload must be considered, as well. Holding a tablet or phone for prolonged periods of time instead of using the hands to carry out tasks in work and play can lead to underdeveloped motor skills and musculoskeletal disorders.[45]

Additionally, many schools teach most or all subjects on laptops, which require typing on a keyboard. However, this means that writing by hand is used drastically less in the classroom, and teachers report that Gen Alpha students struggle to even write their own names in fifth grade.[46] Handwriting is important for cognitive development, memory, motor skills, and reading.[47] Due to mobile-device usage, there has also been an increase in postural defects. These postural deficiencies, which are reported in young children and adults, can even change the spine over time.[48]

Recent reports show that children are also struggling with basic fine-motor tasks, like zipping coats, turning book pages, or using scissors—skills that were once second nature in early childhood. A 2025 survey found that 77 percent of teachers reported increased difficulty with pencil and scissor use, and 69 percent noted more students struggling to tie their shoes compared to five years ago. Educators have observed that many Gen Alpha students arrive at school unable to stack blocks or hold a spoon properly. Experts attribute this decline to a combination of increased screen time, reduced outdoor play, and a shift toward convenience in parenting—such as stretchy pants instead of buttons and prepackaged snacks that eliminate the need for utensils.[49] These changes, while practical, deprive children of opportunities to build essential motor skills through everyday tasks.

Visuals—Not Text

Generation Alpha lives in a "visually intense" world.[50] Researchers and educators suggest that Gen Alpha will be more receptive to visual learning, not text, to mimic what they see on their tablets and other screens.[51] A 2024 article on how Generation Alpha learns put it this way: "Make it visual, make it interactive, or make it disappear."[52]

Visual literacy (VL) is defined as a group of skills that help one to understand content via images. Generation Alpha's visual literacy sits at very high levels, and teachers who put content into infographics or any other kind of visual will likely receive positive results. According to Pınar Nuhoğlu Kibar, visual content for young learners can be "static" (an unanimated visual) or an augmented reality (AR)/virtual reality (VR) environment.[53] As they continue to advance, there will be more opportunities to integrate immersive technologies like AR and VR into piano teaching.

YouTube has become a major educational resource for children today, offering everything from the alphabet to coding tutorials. Given Generation Alpha's comfort and familiarity with YouTube, it's a great idea to guide them toward valuable content. Recommend educational YouTube channels or even create and share your own content for them to explore. They will appreciate and enjoy this engaging form of learning.

Strengths of Gen Alpha Piano Students

Generation Alpha is still very young, so there is limited research on this population, which may make the challenges of today's society seem more prominent. However, the admirable qualities of this younger generation have not been overlooked. This section highlights these great traits of Generation Alpha and provides tips on how to leverage them in a piano-studio setting.

Logical Thinking

Kids of today are said to be adept at using logical reasoning and are considered very level-headed. Gen Alpha is good at making inferences, meaning that their deductive thinking is at a high level. They are also strategic thinkers, which is always a plus in any setting.[54] Giving our Gen Alpha students the chance to engage in critical thinking and providing them problems to solve on their own will help sharpen those skills that already show potential. Furthermore, giving students challenges to solve with their peers can teach them collaborative problem-solving.[55]

Awareness

Today's children are more exposed to technology than any previous generation at their age. Generation Alpha is highly aware of issues in their neighborhoods and communities, and they likely already recognize these problems as worth addressing and solving. They are less sheltered in this regard compared to previous generations. Generation Alpha also possesses a problem-solving mentality, shaped by their awareness of global issues. While Gen Z often focuses on raising awareness through protests, Generation Alpha tends to have more realistic views and a logical perspective on how to overcome challenges.

Digital Intelligence

Generation Alpha has a high DQ, and no, that doesn't mean Dairy Queen! DQ was coined in 2006 and means digital intelligence quotient.[56] This skill is the "ability to adapt emotions, behaviors, credential to cope with digital life."[57] Generation Alpha still has room for growth in certain areas, but they are already proficient in many aspects of DQ. According to the 2019 DQ Global Standards Report, there are eight broad areas of DQ:

1 **Digital Identity:** the ability to build a wholesome online and offline identity
2 **Digital Use:** the ability to use technology in a balanced, healthy, and civic way
3 **Digital Safety:** the ability to understand, mitigate, and manage various cyber risks through safe, responsible, and ethical use of technology
4 **Digital Security:** the ability to detect, avoid, and manage different levels of cyber threats to protect data, devices, networks, and systems
5 **Digital Emotional Intelligence:** the ability to recognize, navigate, and express emotions in one's intra- and interpersonal interactions
6 **Digital Communication:** the ability to communicate and collaborate with others using technology
7 **Digital Literacy:** the ability to find, read, evaluate, synthesize, create, adapt, and share info, media, and technology
8 **Digital Rights:** the ability to understand and uphold human rights when using technology[58]

Generation Alpha excels in point 7, digital literacy! If you guide your Gen Alpha student in the right direction, they will quickly and effectively use digital tools to their advantage, combining them with their creativity. For instance, you can introduce them to apps, backing tracks, and recording capabilities and demonstrate some basic functions. They will grasp these tools and start using them proficiently in no time.

The book *The Teacher of Generation Alpha* encourages educators to integrate digital tools into their teaching, as this approach represents the future of education. Students will adapt quickly and favorably to these tools, enhancing their learning experience. This advice bodes well for piano instructors, as well. By continuously exploring new horizons in digital pedagogical advances, we can inspire our students to also adopt this mindset. It is important to always think outside the box and consider how digital tools, even those not directly related to music, can be used to benefit piano instruction. While the influx of new tools, like AR and AI, can be overwhelming, it's also an incredibly exciting time in history. We have the privilege of being part of this technological evolution!

Notes

1. Ana Peréz Marco, "Generation Z Piano Students: Characteristics and Educational Approach," *Ana Marco* (blog), November 22, 2022, https://www.anamarcopianist.com/post/generation-z-piano-students-characteristics-and-educational-approach.
2. Sebastian Deterding, Dan Dixon, Rilla Khaled, and Lennart Nacke, "From Game Design Elements to Gamefulness: Defining 'Gamification,'" paper presented at the fifteenth International Academic MindTrek Conference, "Envisioning Future Media Environments," September 2011, 9–15.
3. Othman Mohd Noor Azman, Mas Anom Abdul Rashid, Ida Rosnita Ismail, Mohd Faiq Abd Aziz, Norizan Saifulrizan, and Sarah Artikah Mohamad Saad, "Predicting Preferred Learning Styles on Teaching Approaches Among Gen Z Visual Learner," *Turkish Journal of Computer and Mathematics Education* 12, no. 9 (2021): 2969–78, https://turcomat.org/index.php/turkbilmat/article/view/4711/3994.
4. Chih-Hao Lin, "Use Progressive Visualization Teaching Method to Improve Learning Motivation of Calculus Courses," *European Journal of Social and Behavioural Sciences* 31, no. 2 (April 2022): 92–110, https://www.europeanpublisher.com/en/article/10.15405/ejsbs.315.
5. Darla Rothman, "A Tsunami of Learners Called Generation Z" (paper, West Virginia University Continuing and Professional Education, 2016), https://ce.wvu.edu/media/15624/needs-different_learning_styles.pdf.
6. "Spot the Difference: Brain Changes That Enable Fine Visual Discrimination Learning," National Eye Institute, July 8, 2022, https://www.nei.nih.gov/about/news-and-events/news/spot-difference-brain-changes-enable-fine-visual-discrimination-learning.

7. Wendy Kopp, "Five Education Shifts That Will Enable a Better Future," *Teach for All Blog* (blog), September 15, 2021, https://medium.com/teach-for-all-blog/five-education-shifts-that-will-enable-a-better-future-b074ce451742.
8. Miguel Muniz Calvente, Adrian Álvarez-Vázquez, and Pelayo Fernandez, "Collaborative Learning Through Youtube," *Journal of Higher Education Theory and Practice* 22, no. 7 (2022): 202–8, https://doi.org/10.33423/jhetp.v22i7.5284.
9. David Crystal, "Texting," *ELT Journal* 62, no. 1 (January 2008): 77–83, https://doi.org/10.1093/elt/ccm080.
10. Adnan Olia, "Text Message Trends and Statistics You Should Know in 2024 (and Beyond!)," *Email Archiving Blog* (blog), accessed October 15, 2025, https://www.intradyn.com/text-message-statistics-trends/; "Total Number of SMS and MMS Messages Sent in the United States from 2005 to 2021," Statista, accessed June 13, 2025, https://www.statista.com/statistics/185879/number-of-text-messages-in-the-united-states-since-2005/.
11. Monty Benfica, "Gen Z Girl Struggles to Focus on Events Overseas Without Subway Surfer Gameplay Below Coverage," *Betoota Advocate*, accessed October 15, 2025, https://www.betootaadvocate.com/breaking-news/gen-z-girl-struggles-to-focus-on-events-overseas-without-subway-surfer-gameplay-below-coverage/.
12. Özlem Ömür, "Characteristics of Generation Z Piano Students from the Perspective of Piano Teachers," *International Journal of Education and Literacy Studies* 9, no. 4 (October 2021): 278–85, https://journals.aiac.org.au/index.php/IJELS/article/view/6963; Shefaly Shorey, Daria Vyugina, Natalia Waechter, and Nina Dolev, "Communication Preferences and Behaviors," in *Gen Z Around the World: Understanding the Global Cohort Culture of Generation Z*, ed. Corey Seemiller and Meghan Grace, 31–42 (Emerald, 2024), https://doi.org/10.1108/978-1-83797-092-620241004.
13. Kathleen A. J. Mohr and Eric S. Mohr, "Understanding Generation Z Students to Promote a Contemporary Learning Environment," *Journal on Empowering Teaching Excellence* 1, no. 1, article 9 (2017): 89, https://doi.org/10.15142/T3M05T.
14. Michael Miller, "Gen Z Is Unlike Any Generation Before It. New Research Sheds Light on Why—and How to Work More Effectively with Zoomers," *Emotional Intelligence at Work*, April 2024, https://www.6seconds.org/2024/04/17/gen-z-state-of-the-heart-research/.
15. Corey Seemiller and Meghan Grace, "Learning Preferences," in *Gen Z Around the World: Understanding the Global Cohort of Generation Z*, ed. Corey Seemiller and Meghan Grace, 69–78 (Emerald, 2024), https://doi.org/10.1108/978-1-83797-092-620241008.
16. Billy Wilson, *Generation Z: Born for the Storm* (Forefront Books, 2021), 34.
17. Melissa De Witte, "What to Know About Gen Z," *Stanford Report*, January 3, 2022, https://news.stanford.edu/stories/2022/01/know-gen-z.
18. Seemiller and Grace, "Learning Preferences," 75.
19. Peter Suciu, "During COVID-19 Outbreak, Can YouTube Help Keep Students Engaged?" *Forbes*, April 9, 2020, https://www.forbes.com/sites/petersuciu/2020/04/09/during-covid-19-outbreak-can-youtube-help-keep-students-engaged/.

20 "Gen Z and Gen Alpha Infographic Update," McCrindle, accessed October 15, 2025, https://mccrindle.com.au/article/topic/generation-z/gen-z-and-gen-alpha-infographic-update/.
21 Karina Ochis, *Gen Z in Work: A Practical Guide to Engaging Employees Across the Generations* (Routledge, 2024), 71, https://doi.org/10.4324/9781032722696.
22 Shorey et al., "Communication Preferences and Behaviors," 40.
23 Ibid.
24 "What Is a Finsta? The Secret World of Fake IG Accounts," Greenlight, January 24, 2024, https://greenlight.com/learning-center/family-safety/what-is-a-finsta.
25 Henry Chandonnet, "Can Facebook Win Back Gen Z?" Fast Company, October 9, 2024, https://www.fastcompany.com/91205088/can-facebook-win-back-gen-z.
26 José Antonio Bowen and C. Edward Watson, *Teaching with AI: A Practical Guide to a New Era of Human Learning* (Johns Hopkins University Press, 2024), 15–16.
27 Shubham Agarwal, "Generation Chatbot," *Business Insider*, February 11, 2025, https://www.businessinsider.com/gen-z-using-ai-chatbots-chatgpt-claude-work-career-jobs-2025-2.
28 Florence Gonsalves, Jama Green, Alex Parrish, Tonia Moxley, Chelsea Seeber, and Ashley Williamson, "AI—The Good, the Bad, and the Scary," *Virginia Tech Engineer*, Fall 2023, https://eng.vt.edu/magazine/stories/fall-2023/ai.html.
29 Hannah Freeman, "Screen Time Negatively Affecting Children During COVID-19," in *Covid-19: Success Within Devastation*, ed. Yang Wu (Clemson University, 2020), https://opentextbooks.clemson.edu/stswu1010fall2020/chapter/technology-negatively-affecting-children-during-covid-19/.
30 "Understanding Generation Alpha," McCrindle, accessed October 15, 2025, https://mccrindle.com.au/article/topic/generation-alpha/generation-alpha-defined/.
31 Ahmet Aydemir, "Teaching Generation Alpha," in *The Teacher of Generation Alpha*, ed. Nihal Yurtseven, 33–42 (Peter Lang, 2020), 35–38.
32 [deleted], "Veteran teacher here, and I agree. In parent teacher conferences, they straight-up tell me they're too tired after work to read with their children...," comment on "There's Been a Lot of Talk Online About Gen Alpha's Terrible Behavior," Reddit, November 16, 2023, https://www.reddit.com/r/Millennials/comments/17wtsv0/theres_been_a_lot_of_talk_online_about_gen_alphas/.
33 Lauren Arundell, Laura Gould, Nicola D. Ridgers, et al., "'Everything Kind of Revolves around Technology': A Qualitative Exploration of Families' Screen Use Experiences, and Intervention Suggestions," *BMC Public Health* 22, no. 1 (2022): 1606, https://doi.org/10.1186/s12889-022-14007-w.
34 Kim I. Mills, host, *Speaking of Psychology*, podcast, episode 189, "Is Technology Killing Empathy? With Sherry Turkle, PhD," May 4, 2022, https://www.apa.org/news/podcasts/speaking-of-psychology/anti-empathy-machine.
35 Lauren Brown West-Rosenthal, "Gen Alpha Isn't a Uniquely Disrespectful Generation—They're Just Misunderstood," *Parents*, updated January 10, 2025, https://www.parents.com/gen-alpha-kids-disrespectful-or-misunderstood-8725182.

36 Jessica Kato, "What Educators Need to Know About Generation Alpha," EdSurge, February 2, 2024, https://www.edsurge.com/news/2024-02-02-what-educators-need-to-know-about-generation-alpha.

37 ketocavegirl, "I'm a millennial single mom to one gen alpha child. I think it's going to depend on a lot of factors but this is what I'm seeing...," comment on "There's Been a Lot of Talk Online about Gen Alpha's Terrible Behavior," Reddit, November 16, 2023, https://www.reddit.com/r/Millennials/comments/17wtsv0/theres_been_a_lot_of_talk_online_about_gen_alphas/.

38 NeuroLaunch Editorial Team, "Gen Alpha Behavior: Navigating the Unique Traits of Digital Native Generation," *NeuroLaunch* (blog), September 22, 2024, https://neurolaunch.com/gen-alpha-behavior/.

39 Anna Gnatyshyna, "Gen Alpha Kids Know More than Us but Need Guidance—Concerning Kids," CNE.news, August 17, 2024, https://cne.news/article/4391-gen-alpha-kids-know-more-than-us-but-need-guidance-concerning-kids.

40 West-Rosenthal, "Gen Alpha."

41 Mika Inokoshi, "Here's another perspective – I find that as a parent there is a culture for kids to 'try' every activity out there ...," reply to Tonya Prince Pruhs, "I am concerned about the future of children. I've noticed for the past 5 years or more that kids aren't as coordinated or as smart as they used to be ...," Facebook, September 29, 2023, https://www.facebook.com/groups/pianoteachercentral/permalink/6398255500304121.

42 Lucas Benjamin, "The Evolution of Exclusivity: Why College Admissions Are More Competitive than Ever," Science Survey, February 12, 2025, https://thesciencesurvey.com/news/2025/02/12/the-evolution-of-exclusivity-why-college-admissions-are-more-competitive-than-ever/.

43 Inokoshi, "Here's another perspective."

44 NeuroLaunch Editorial Team, "Gen Alpha Behavior."

45 Minkyung Lee, Yunkyung Hong, Seunghoon Lee, et al., "The Effects of Smartphone Use on Upper Extremity Muscle Activity and Pain Threshold," *Journal of Physical Therapy Science* 27, no. 6 (2015): 1743–45, https://doi.org/10.1589/jpts.27.1743.

46 Kristen Seo, "Digital Age Sets Gen Alpha Up for Failure in Classroom," *Emory Wheel*, November 20, 2024, https://www.emorywheel.com/article/2024/11/digital-age-sets-gen-alpha-up-for-failure-in-classroom.

47 Marcel E. Baril and Rachel Joy M. Carriaga-Baril, "Penmanship Program Implemented for Generation Alpha Through the Lens of Ochave's ABCD Model," *International Journal of Advanced Multidisciplinary Research and Studies* 4, no. 1 (2024): 219–25, https://www.multiresearchjournal.com/admin/uploads/archives/archive-1704789426.pdf.

48 Paweł Adam Piepora, Justyna Bagińska, Zbigniew Norbert Piepiora, and Jolita Vvwinhardt, "Development or Decline of Physical Culture? Physical Activity of the Alpha Generation from a Polish Perspective," *Health Problems of Civilization* 19, no. 3 (2025): 306–14, https://doi.org/10.5114/hpc.2024.145535.

49. Teal Burrell, "Kids Are Losing Fine Motor Skills—and Screens Might Be to Blame," *National Geographic*, January 28, 2025, https://www.nationalgeographic.com/science/article/why-kids-are-losing-fine-motor-skills.
50. Pınar Nuhoğlu Kibar, "Infographic Creation as an Essential Skill for Highly Visual Gen Alpha," *Journal of Visual Literacy* 43, no. 2 (2024): 67–72, https://doi.org/10.1080/1051144X.2024.2350847.
51. Çigdem Apaydin and Feyza Kaya, "An Analysis of the Preschool Teachers' Views on Alpha Generation," *European Journal of Education Studies* 6, no. 11 (2020): 123–41, https://eric.ed.gov/?id=ED602722.
52. NeuroLaunch Editorial Team, "Gen Alpha Behavior."
53. Kibar, "Infographic Creation."
54. Nihal Yurtseven, ed., *The Teacher of Generation Alpha* (Peter Lang, 2020).
55. Susan Z. Beers, *Teaching 21st Century Skills: An ASCD Action Tool* (Association for Supervision and Curriculum Development, 2011).
56. Jiří Dostál, Xiaojun Wang, William Steingartner, and Prasart Nuangchalerm, "Digital Intelligence—New Concept in Context of Future School of Education," in *Proceedings of ICERI2017 Conference 16th–18th November 2017, Seville, Spain* (September 26, 2018): 3706–12, https://ssrn.com/abstract=3255366.
57. Yurtseven, *Teacher of Generation Alpha.*
58. Yuhyun Park, ed., *DQ Global Standards Report 2019: Common Framework for Digital Literacy, Skills and Readiness* (DQ Institute, 2019), https://www.dqinstitute.org/wp-content/uploads/2019/03/DQGlobalStandardsReport2019.pdf.

6 Fostering Creativity

As a musical art form, the heart of piano playing is a creative process. Experimentation with sound, touch, articulation, tonal colors, pedaling, dynamic levels, and phrasing plays a role in this artistic process. Additional creative musical activities include improvisation and composition. Prior to the heightened interest in achieving virtuosity around the middle of the twentieth century, these two skills were developed as equals alongside pianistic technique. Performers who played the harpsichord, organ, fortepiano, and piano throughout the eighteenth, nineteenth, and early twentieth centuries routinely presented their own compositions. During the baroque period, performers were often expected to improvise, while in the classical era, it was customary for them to compose and perform their own cadenzas in concertos.

Unfortunately, by the mid-twentieth century, the common practices of improvisation and composition were no longer seen as essential to the standard piano lesson, and instruction focused on playing existing repertoire. As a result, many people in the field started to segregate these proficiencies as separate abilities or talents that only certain people possessed or felt drawn to. Grounded in classical Western art music, traditional piano lessons were seen as a space where students played technical exercises and drills, learned how to read notation, studied repertoire from the four (maybe five) musical eras, and followed the rules. Improvisation was viewed as something jazz players did, and composition was relegated to only the experts.

However, in the last twenty-five years or so, there has been a resurgence of interest in incorporating these important skills into standard piano education to provide a holistic experience for students. Stereotypically, the general public may consider traditional piano lessons to be arduous, dull, and boring—and to some degree, they are right! The piano-teaching world has acknowledged that perhaps we as instructors have been more focused on regurgitating the same repertoire, the same technical exercises, and the same musical solutions. Therefore, there has been a shift toward more inclusion of creative activity in piano study to spark greater interest in students and to make piano playing a more meaningful and personal experience for each person. As a part of this process, everything old is new again, and improvisation and composition are seeing a revival in piano education as a means to enhance creative thought.

Reframing Creative Thinking

The notions surrounding creativity, however, can sometimes feel rather elitist. General society tends to gravitate to the thought that only certain people are creative—those who are the risk-takers, those who can think outside the box, and those who can come up with big ideas.[1] However, that is not always the case. Every single person has the capacity to be creative in ways that are attainable and meaningful for them. Furthermore, there are many people in the piano world who think they cannot improvise or compose. Trying this "new" type of activity may seem overwhelming and somewhat frightening. This does not need to be the case. In this chapter, we reimagine creativity.

In his article "Musical Imagination: Perception and Production, Beauty and Creativity," David Hargreaves states, "Imagination is also the essence of the creative perception of music."[2] Artists can flex their imagination capabilities by reorganizing or simplifying past impressions to create new ideas. Forging these new relationships between existing concepts forms novel thoughts. Hargreaves has a particularly accessible and inviting approach to thinking about creativity: "Rather than seeing it [creativity] as a generalized capacity of individuals, it can be seen as producing solutions to specific problems in specific situations."[3] In essence, creative thought can emerge in small and manageable chunks, and it can exist in a variety of forms.

In 2020, Robert Weisberg wrote the book *Rethinking Creativity: Inside-the-Box Thinking as the Basis for Innovation*. He explains that for something to be considered creative, the general thought is that it needs to be novel and of value. Determining if something is of value often involves outside people who directly or indirectly verify if something is creative. For example, art gallery owners, concert venues, producers, and an appreciative public all have a role in determining if an endeavor is creative or not, and they end up being gatekeepers for the category of creativity. The inherent problem is that sometimes these gatekeepers may disagree—something that is creative for one party might not be creative for the other. Furthermore, something that feels novel for an individual might not be novel for society. Nevertheless, it can still be a creative expression.[4]

It is important for students to engage in creative activity regularly, as it puts them in a state of *flow*. The concept of flow was coined by psychologist Mihaly Csikszentmihalyi in the 1970s and refers to a mental state in which an individual is fully immersed in an activity with heightened focus, involvement, and enjoyment.[5] Csikszentmihalyi also identified characteristics of a creative personality. Table 6.1 highlights the fact that creativity can stem from different scenarios and environments.

If our students learn to understand what flow feels like, then they will encounter more freedom to connect with the art of playing the piano, making it a more personal and profound opportunity for personal expression. When in flow, students don't stop to correct mistakes; they bask in the glow of complete enjoyment. Take note that there is a difference between enjoyment and pleasure. Being in flow requires high levels of concentration. Some activities are more likely to induce flow for certain students, and teachers should be cognizant of these moments so that they can focus on these types of activities.[6]

Table 6.1 Characteristics of the Creative Personality

Energetic but quiet and at rest
Smart yet naïve
Playful but disciplined
Imaginative while rooted in a sense of reality
Extroverted and introverted
Humble and proud
Generally nonconforming for rigid gender stereotypes
Rebellious and conservative
Passionate and objective
Open and sensitive, making them vulnerable to suffering and pain but also significant enjoyment

When designing activities for students to spark creativity, it is important to remember that they don't need to be complicated. If improvisation, even in a structured format, seems overwhelming for the student (or even the teacher), remember that imaginative listening is also a creative activity. There are three determinants of listening responses: the music, the listening environment, and the listener. It is important to think about how networks of association can heighten imaginative listening:

1 **Musical Reference:** How does this piece of music relate to the music I already know?
2 **Cultural Associations:** Does the music fit within the typical context where this music is usually heard?
3 **Personal Associations:** What does this music mean to me?

We explore specific listening activities in chapters 8 and 9 that are simple solutions for inciting creative responses with our students.

A Holistic Approach

Now, let us pause for a moment and think about some characteristics of our two generations of piano students and how this knowledge can guide teachers in nurturing their creativity. Studies and observations of Generations Z and Alpha conclude that they enjoy individualized learning and experiences. They are adept with technology and have grown up in the digital age. Additionally, Gen Z places strong emphasis on self-care, and both Gen Z and Gen Alpha need to find healthy outlets for their heightened anxiety; students need art more than ever.

Creativity is essential in today's world, where the constant influx of information often leaves little room for original thought. Martha Beck in her book *Beyond Anxiety* discusses some real truths about the benefits of creativity and how curiosity and exploration can combat the high levels of anxiety we see in our world today.[7] She explains that we are living in an unprecedented world. Almost every global and national issue seems historic, especially for young minds still developing their understanding of the world. One worthy solution for managing this distress is to unlock the power of one's right brain and let it take more control of the cognitive process. Creativity is the product of our right brain, and the feelings and thoughts in a rush of creativity differ greatly from those in an anxiety episode. Therefore, it is fair to say that "creativity is the opposite of anxiety."[8] Creativity shifts your mindset from needing to control every outcome to being open to the unknown. It invites you to step into a space of wonder, where questions matter more than answers and where uncertainty becomes a path to insight rather than a source of fear. In this way, creativity transforms anxiety into curiosity and control into connection—with yourself, with others, and with the world around you.

What do these findings and ideas mean for us as teachers? Let's break all of this down into a holistic Venn diagram that connects music making at the piano, other art forms, and technology with the goal of providing as many creative outlets and artistic enrichment and experience as possible (see figure 6.1). This well-integrated perspective can inspire students to explore other art forms and provide extra creative outlets as a form of self-care. The relationship with technology also provides an opportunity to use a tool

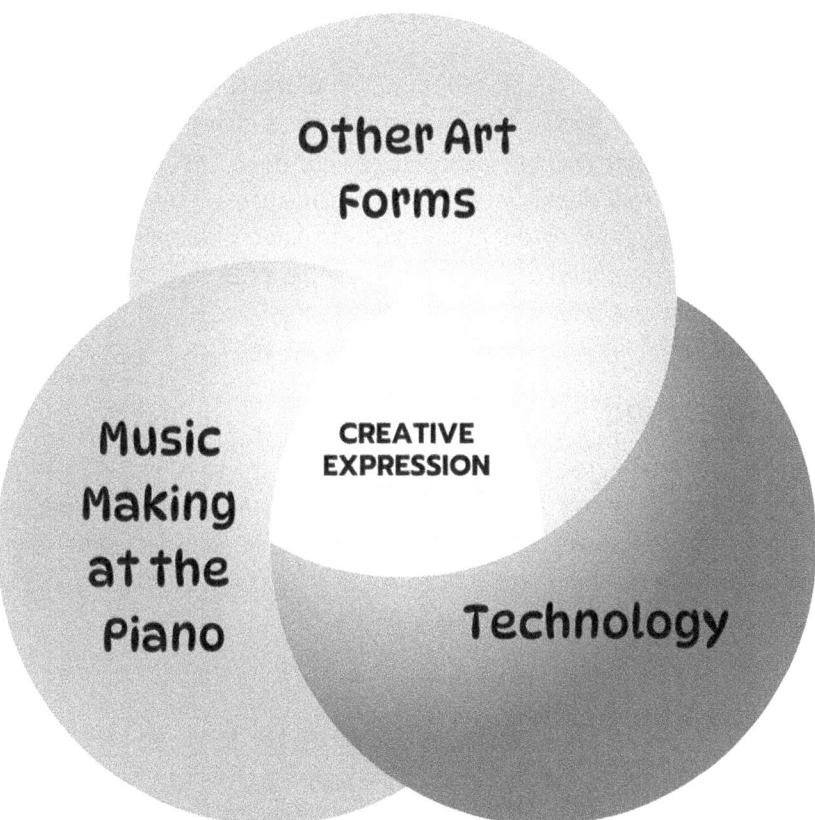

Figure 6.1 The interrelation of technology, music making at the piano, and other art forms within creative expression. *Illustration by the author.*

that both generations are comfortable with and use every day and shows students your adaptation and willingness to use items from their world.

This triangular relationship is effective for these reasons:

1. **Digital Natives:** These generations are fluent in technology and expect interactivity and personalization.
2. **Multimodal Learners:** Gen Z and Gen Alpha thrive when learning is visual, auditory, and kinesthetic.
3. **Creativity as Identity:** Both generations value self-expression and authenticity, making creative exploration essential.

While each of the three components stands well on its own, they also intersect and enhance one another, as illustrated in the following discussion.

Music Making at the Piano

The piano should be embraced as a powerful medium for self-expression and creativity. Our goal is not merely to have students replicate existing compositions but to encourage them to develop their own expressive voices. We want them to feel empowered—active participants in their own musical journey. As educators, it is our responsibility to equip students with the tools and guidance they need to explore, create, and express themselves through music. (See chapter 9 for specific strategies.)

Improvisation

Improvisation gives students freedom to explore the keys and learn about what sounds they can create. This can also include free play time (especially beneficial for younger students). Call-and-response activities can also be productive for teaching students to think in terms of producing simple sounds and melodies at the piano.

Composition and Songwriting

Composing gives students a sense of pride, joy, and freedom when we give them the practical tools for transferring ideas to sounds. Even a four-measure composition by a student will give them a sense of satisfaction. Composition is not just for the elite, polished musician!

Expressive Interpretation

Encourage students to experiment with expressive ideas and connect them to vivid analogies. Allow time for exploration—diving into the nuances of dynamics, expressive contrasts, and tone color—to help them develop a deeper, more personal connection to the music.

Collaborative Music Making

Involving students in duets, ensembles, and accompaniment not only sharpens their listening and timing skills, but it also fosters meaningful social connections. These collaborative experiences offer students an additional musical skill set—one they may choose to pursue further, whether in academic settings or simply for the joy and fulfillment of making music with others.

Repertoire Choices

Give students the opportunity to choose pieces that reflect their personal interests, and prioritize a diverse range of genres—jazz, contemporary, world music, and beyond. Even a small investment of time in this area can yield significant rewards in engagement and growth. Additionally, it's valuable for teachers to continually expand their own musical awareness, both for personal enrichment and for thoughtful programming in future performances.

Multimodal Learning

Visual Arts

Children are inherently multimodal learners and combine different forms of expression. They may sing and dance, tell stories while drawing pictures, build models to explain their ideas, use gestures and facial expressions to convey emotions, or act out scenarios during imaginative play.[9] Education researchers have discovered that when children combine music listening with drawing or painting, they are more likely to have a better understanding of the music's form and greater insight into the emotional content of the piece. When they are asked to draw pictures based on different repertoire, their visual responses reflect the music. Defined variances in the drawings show that children truly listen to and recognize changes in musical styles. In a 2019 study on this topic, Rivka Elkoshi found that pieces with symmetrical forms elicited drawings that also demonstrated regularity and less-unique features.[10] She also cites previous literature indicating children consistently associate certain colors or color families with high and low sounds.

Using drawing, painting, and other representations of visual art in the piano lesson can reap many benefits. It has been shown that the use of color can help students understand the intricacies of musical notation. The creation of musical graphics can be very stimulating for youngsters, especially when teachers encourage freedom of thought. In essence, the use of visual creations can be a form of invented notation.[11] Teachers may even want to consider asking beginner students to create and establish their own symbols and visual images of the sounds they hear prior to introducing them to traditional notation. In doing so, students are actively engaged in interpreting and assigning meaning to the various sounds based on their own experiences.[12]

Through this mode of learning, students can acquire deeper insight regarding music structure and music terminology. Through drawing and painting, children can learn to identify representations, symbols, and signs. Visual expression can be a great starting point for composition. After a student creates a picture, the shapes, outlines, and colors of the drawing can inspire pitch and rhythm. Then they can experiment with sounds at the piano to aurally and musically manifest the essence of their creative visualization. It is also important to converse with students about their drawings in order to encourage self-reflection. This will create a stronger emotional connection with their visual and musical artistic expressions.[13] What they say about their drawings is important.[14]

A compelling example of a long-term interdisciplinary project is organizing a recital where students create original artwork inspired by their musical pieces. These visual interpretations are then projected during the performance, creating a dynamic fusion of visual and musical expression. Salem, Oregon's chapter of Music Teachers National Association (MTNA) holds such an event, the Art and Music Festival. One could also collaborate with a local art studio where the art students draw or paint illustrations for piano students' pieces and attend the recital to listen to the music they have helped bring to life through their art.

Movement

Since the beginning of time, music and movement have served as fundamental means of expression, allowing humans to convey emotions and connect with one another across cultures and epochs.[15] Music and dance are referred to as "sister arts." In some languages, the words for dance and music are even used interchangeably.[16] Different methods, such as those by Carl Orff, Zoltán Kodály, and Émile Jacques-Dalcroze, incorporate movement as a major building block of their method. According to the Dalcroze Society of America, using movement alongside music education develops a stronger sense of rhythm and harmony, unlocks easier and more expressive performance, heightens listening skills and intuition, and makes music easier to understand through the body.

Renowned music educator Edwin Gordon developed the Music Learning Theory (MLT) and stated that rhythm must be processed not only intellectually but also through the body.[17] MLT has been adopted for piano pedagogy by such teachers as Marilyn Lowe, who, in cooperation with Gordon, developed the Music Moves for Piano series based on his teaching. Lowe encourages activities that distinguish between weighted and free gestures, engaging different parts of the body to enhance awareness of physical mechanisms involved in piano playing. MLT has helped to reignite the productive use of rote teaching in piano pedagogy, and in recent years, the field has seen an increase in the publication of books focused on this approach.

Technology

Even without this book, you probably could have guessed that Gen Z and Gen Alpha students are more comfortable with the technology and tools of the digital age than previous generations. While all tools have their pros and cons, technology can help to develop creativity and even merge some of the areas discussed earlier in this chapter. Technology continues to evolve, and brilliant ideas for programs and apps that boost user imagination and innovation are in constant development. An article titled "What Is Creative Technology?" asserts that technology programmed with a vision for creative use can "enhance and augment traditional modes of expression."[18] Universities are even offering degree programs titled Creative Technologies, which use digital tools to complement and enrich such disciplines as art, creative writing, film, and music.[19]

Composition and Technology

Incorporating technology into music lessons can open exciting pathways for creativity and self-expression. Tools like GarageBand, BandLab, and Soundtrap offer user-friendly platforms where students can begin composing, layering sounds, and experimenting with musical ideas—even with little to no prior experience.

These digital tools allow students to explore rhythm, harmony, and structure in a hands-on way, making composition feel accessible and fun. Additionally, using YouTube backing tracks—such as drumbeats or chord progressions—can provide a rich, supportive backdrop for improvisation. Whether in lessons or at home, these accompaniments help fill the musical space, making improvisation more engaging and musically satisfying. See chapter 9 for more detail on tools to use with students. Encouraging students to explore these platforms not only builds their compositional skills but also fosters confidence and independence in their musical journey.

Gamification

The practice of engaging in play has historically been viewed as both a method of instruction and a crucial environment for early education. Plato viewed play as a formative experience, shaping children's ability to navigate social dynamics and professional paths later in life. Incorporating games into instructional activity offers teachers the chance to introduce or review material with students in a fun and amusing manner. Learners are able to interact with the content in new ways and view content from different perspectives.[20]

The modern-day manifestation of play is gaming, an activity enjoyed by both Generations Z and Alpha students. Digital games, including *Roblox*, *Fortnite*, and *Minecraft*, are often highly immersive, capable of capturing users' attention for extended periods of time. These games have the ability to put players in the state of flow, which is why they are so appealing to play. These types of games are usually viewed as something people do for leisure, however researchers have explored the qualities that make them so engaging and how these elements can be effectively integrated into educational environments.[21]

An example of educational media that blends learning with gamelike features is the popular app *Duolingo*. This app introduces users to different languages in ways that are personalized, motivating, and fun. The use of streaks and rewards encourages players to keep playing and improve their progress. In light of growing concerns about declining attention spans, gamification is increasingly recognized as an effective strategy for sustaining student engagement.[22] The Karyn Purvis Institute of Child Development states that play in learning has many benefits for the brain, as it promotes cognitive development (e.g., problem-solving and collaboration) while removing barriers to cognitive development, such as anxiety and stress.[23] Furthermore, because effective games have the ability to put users in a state of flow, they can serve as a gateway to inspire creativity.

It can be helpful to see how researchers have categorized the characteristics of gaming so that teachers can look at ways they can effectively gamify elements of their lessons. The workings of games can be organized into three hierarchical categories: dynamics, mechanics, and components.[24] Figure 6.2 describes each of these three groups.

Furthermore, gamified learning harbors the following attributes:

- It is intrinsically motivating because the rules end up being part of decision-making processes. The rules do not stifle choice.
- This type of educational experience is fun because students can see the results of their efforts.
- There is an authenticity associated with this educational experience. Students can test their abilities without significant ramifications in real life.
- Through feedback and correction, students develop independence.
- Gamification of learning is experiential.[25]

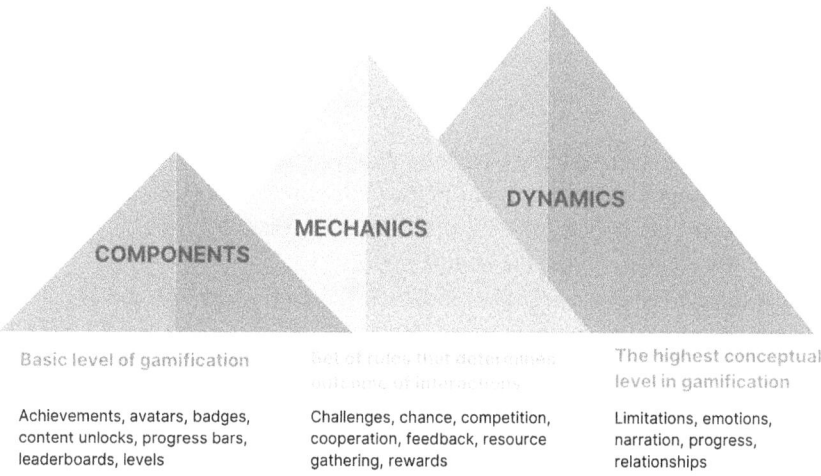

Figure 6.2 Three gaming categories. *Illustration by the author.*

By identifying these elements of gamification, piano teachers can find alternative approaches for introducing concepts that have typically been seen as dry and uninteresting. This knowledge can also help instructors determine which gamified education media (such as which apps) are best suited for their students.

We hope that this chapter demystifies the concept of creativity and dispels the notion that it is relegated to an elite group of high-level thinkers. Creativity is an innate part of being human. With the right approach, anyone can unlock and nurture their creative potential.

Notes

1. Jonathan Kladder and William Lee, "Music Teachers Perceptions of Creativity: A Preliminary Investigation," *Creativity Research Journal* 31, no. 4 (2019): 401, https://doi.org/10.1080/10400419.2019.1651189.
2. David J. Hargreaves, "Musical Imagination: Perception and Production, Beauty and Creativity," *Psychology of Music* 40, no. 5 (September 2012): 539, https://doi.org/10.1177/0305735612444893.
3. Ibid., 545.
4. Robert W. Weisberg, *Rethinking Creativity: Inside-the-Box Thinking as the Basis for Innovation* (Cambridge University Press, 2020).
5. Mihaly Csikszentmihalyi, *Flow: The Psychology of Optimal Experience* (Harper & Row, 1990).
6. Lucy Green, *Music, Informal Learning and the School: A New Classroom Pedagogy* (Routledge, 2008), 84.
7. Martha Beck, *Beyond Anxiety: Curiosity, Creativity and Finding Your Life's Purpose* (Little, Brown, 2025), 107–202.
8. Ibid., 114.
9. Roger Mantie and Beatriz Ilari, "'He Sings with Rhythm; He Is from India': Children's Drawings and the Music Classroom," in *The Oxford Handbook of Philosophical and Qualitative Assessment in Music Education*, ed. David J. Elliott, Marissa Silverman, and Gary E. McPherson (Oxford University Press, 2019), 368.
10. Rivka Elkoshi, "When Sounds, Colors, and Shapes Meet: Investigating Children's Audiovisual Art in Response to Classical Music," *International Journal of Music Education* 37, no. 4 (November 2019): 586, https://doi.org/10.1177/0255761419866084.
11. Ibid., 577.
12. Johanna Maria Roels and Peter Van Petegem, "The Integration of Visual Expression in Music Education for Children," *British Journal of Music Education* 31, no. 3 (November 2014): 298, https://doi.org/10.1017/S0265051714000163.

13 Ibid., 313.
14 Mantie and Ilari, "'He Sings with Rhythm,'" 368.
15 Beau Sievers, Larry Polansky, Michael Casey, and Thalia Wheatley, "Music and Movement Share a Dynamic Structure That Supports Universal Expressions of Emotion," *Proceedings of the National Academy of Sciences of the United States of America* 110, no. 1 (January 2, 2013): 70–75, https://doi.org/10.1073/pnas.1209023110.
16 John Blacking, *How Musical Is Man?* (University of Washington Press, 1973).
17 Edwin Gordon, *Learning Sequences in Music: A Contemporary Music Learning Theory*, rev. ed. (GIA, 2012), 38–39.
18 "What Is Creative Technology?" Meadows School of the Arts, Southern Methodist University, October 19, 2023, https://www.smu.edu/meadows/newsandevents/news/2023/what-is-creative-technology.
19 "Creative Technologies," Thomas University, accessed October 17, 2025, https://www.thomasu.edu/creative-technologies/.
20 Diana Dumlavwalla, Melody Morrison, and Ricardo Pozenatto, "Fresh Vibes: Connecting with Generation Z and Alpha Students in Your Modern Music Studio," in *Proceedings of NCKP 2023: The Piano Conference* (Frances Clark Center, 2024).
21 Ibid.
22 Jan Miškov, "The Place of Gamification in Education," in *Handbook of Research on the Influence and Effectiveness of Gamification in Education*, ed. Antonio Carrizo Moreira, Vanessa Amorim, and Oscar Bernardes (IGI Global, 2022), 4.
23 Sheri Parris and Christian Hernandez, "The Benefits of Play in Cognitive Development," Karyn Purvis Institute for Child Development, accessed June 20, 2025, https://child.tcu.edu/play/#sthash.qc31RVMx.dpbs
24 Miškov, "Place of Gamification," 5.
25 Ibid.

7 Understanding Their Musical Tastes

One factor that contributes to a person's individuality is their musical taste or preference. Every person has a unique set of musical ideals they gravitate toward. Different styles of music affect individuals in a variety of ways. Any piece can elicit a range of emotions, such as joy, fury, anxiety, hope, excitement, optimism, despair, and affection. What draws a person in can define their musical preferences or tastes. An understanding of one's own musical taste can help individuals have a greater understanding of themselves and their development of musical preferences is linked to identity formation.[1] While previously it was assumed that our musical preferences are genetic, recent research indicates that there are more factors that play a role in influencing our musical tastes.

Let's start by looking at what musical taste and preference are and how they are identified. Music psychologists and other researchers who study the perception of music have created many theories. We, the authors, don't feel our field of specialty allows us to conclusively analyze and compare all these theories. However, we draw on some interesting suppositions and generalized inferences that offer helpful insight into how our own musical tastes and those of our students are formed. Furthermore, it is important to acknowledge that there is no single theory that can predict musical preferences accurately.[2]

What Influences Our Musical Tastes and Preferences?

Our preferences are shaped by a number of elements including biology, culture, training, and experiences. Also, although the terms *musical taste* and *musical preference* may be used interchangeably, there is a distinction between the two. *Musical taste* implies a long-term commitment, while *musical preference* refers to what one enjoys at one moment in time and in a specific situation.[3] As we listen to music throughout our lives, we identify our preferences based on individual pieces and songs we hear and that leads to our affinity with certain genres. Our preferences also shift and refine as we age, ultimately creating a personalized collection that reflects our evolving musical taste.[4]

One study identified that personality, as well as personal and cultural values, are predictors of musical taste.[5] Although these factors did not achieve a perfect prediction score, they reliably guided researchers toward accurately predicting participants' musical tastes. Other research has shown that alternate individual differences, including age, gender, and income, may have more influence when predicting musical taste.[6]

Another commonly recognized factor influencing musical preferences is an individual's social environment. Many of us have heard the idiom "Birds of a feather flock together." Parents concerned about the music their children are listening to may be quick to scrutinize their child's close circle of friends as a potential influence. However, this is not always the case. One study looked at peer influence within an online social network and found that friends with similar tastes do not necessarily influence one another; it is the reason they became friends in the first place and maintained the friendship. In fact, the researchers discovered that sharing similar musical tastes was a stronger predictor of friendship than having other common interests.[7] Those who find friends with similar musical tastes enjoy stronger in-group identity, and close relationships can lead to the discovery of new music.[8] As teachers, we may consider harnessing the power of discovering new things, new ideas, and new music in groups.

Cultural context also plays a large role in shaping aesthetic responses to music. For example, Western music relies heavily on the relationship and tension between consonance and dissonance. People growing up in Western countries expect to hear this type of sound and often use these expectations when deciding whether they like a piece of music. Ethnomusicologists compared the responses of participants from the Tsimané, a native Amazonian society with minimal exposure to Western culture, to those of participants from Bolivia and the United States, who had more diverse cultural experiences. The researchers discovered that the Tsimané participants rated consonant and dissonant chords as equally pleasant, while the US and Bolivian participants demonstrated significant preference for consonance. The participants from the Tsimané society still had the ability to aurally discriminate between these different sounds, however they were not influenced to favor consonance because their culture did not demonstrate a bias or preference for that type of sound.[9] This suggests that culture can truly play a dominant role in shaping our responses to music.

The level of musical complexity also affects a person's preferences. There are a couple of theories that effectively illustrate this. Walker's Hedgehog Theory (1980) claims that each individual possesses an internal optimal complexity threshold. If a person finds a piece of music too complex, then they figuratively curl up into a ball and withdraw from listening. In essence, if the music is too difficult for the person to understand or relate to, then their preference for that music is negatively affected. On the flip side, if the level of complexity is too far from the optimal threshold (meaning the music is too easy), then again, the person will stop listening.[10]

Berlyne's Inverted *U* Theory (1971) also effectively illustrates the relationship between musical familiarity and complexity and liking. Overly familiar music may be considered less complex and less engaging. As complexity increases, so does listener interest—up to an optimal point at the peak of the inverted *U*. Beyond this point, if the music is too complex, then enjoyment declines, reflecting a drop on the other side of the curve. Therefore, based on this theory, moderate complexity is most preferred.[11]

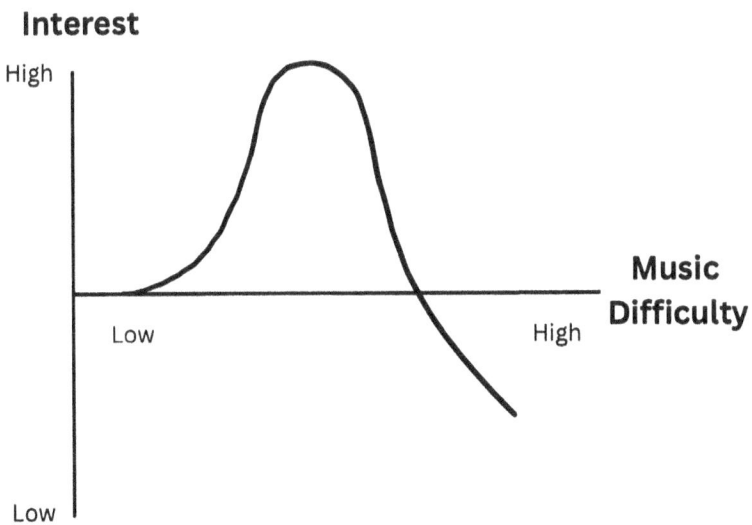

Figure 7.1 Inverted U diagram showing relationship between student interest and music difficulty. *Illustration by the author.*

While excessive familiarity of a musical selection can cause less engagement, it can also reduce perceived complexity, thereby increasing the level of preference. For example, repetition can modify preferences by simplifying complicated music.[12] It can also contribute to the perception of emotion.[13] By boosting exposure, apparent complexity can potentially be decreased, and interest, increased. Consequently, repertoire that may initially seem uninteresting and inaccessible due to its complexity, with increased exposure, can evolve into music the listener comes to appreciate and enjoy. This means that through instruction and mindful attention, musical taste can be enhanced and broadened. Individuals can learn how to hear musical details through various nuances, recognizing form and identifying connections with factual information. Highly engaged listeners show stronger and broader musical preferences.[14] Through education, exposure to a wider range of music can also expand musical preferences. Moreover, verbalizing aspects of music can enhance cognitive processing by encouraging listeners to actively identify and interpret musical elements, demonstrating their capacity to perceive and understand musical detail.[15]

Authority can also influence musical preference, depending on the style period.[16] Approvals and disapprovals can affect preference, along with appropriate and inappropriate modeling.[17] In the context of piano teaching, this underlines the great responsibility that instructors possess and must be mindful of when interacting with their students.

Childhood influences can have a significant impact on our musical preferences and are formed primarily through impregnation (passive exposure) and then inculcation (active teaching).[18] These formative years are also a time when positive musical identities can be established through the involvement of parents as well as the encouragement of family and teachers.[19]

Age can influence not only a person's musical preferences but also how they use music in daily life, such as for social connection, mood regulation, or reminiscing.[20] Members of a generation often have similar musical tastes because they all grew up surrounded by the same types of music. Musical taste can be seen as a social badge for group membership.[21] Take, for example, the height of the boy-band age in the 1990s. Groups like New Kids on the Block, the Backstreet Boys, and NSYNC were all the rage for millennials. We are now seeing a resurgence of these bands, with their current tours aimed at bringing back nostalgia and memories for this generation. Nowadays,

Taylor Swift is seen as the artist who speaks to Gen Z and Gen Alpha, with her relatable lyrics and storytelling. People tend to have a favorable view of others who share their musical tastes. There is a sense of kinship in this connection, which may help explain why generational stereotypes persist.

Musical Preferences of Gen Z and Gen Alpha Students

This leads us to explore the musical preferences of Gen Z and Gen Alpha students. While colloquially it may seem like they only listen to artists like Taylor Swift, Harry Styles, Billie Eilish, and Olivia Rodrigo, their musical tastes are actually very eclectic. One study highlights the responses of thirty-two Gen Z women interviewed in focus groups.[22] While this is a very small sample size, it does provide us with some insight regarding their perspectives.

The participants stated that they liked "anything and everything" and preferences depended on their mood. They also stated that they were not in favor of or crazy about the current music scene and found the lyrical content increasingly inappropriate. They noted a lack of female representation among artists and wanted to see more diversity and inclusion of gender in the musicians promoted.

Another important point they brought up is how they access music—through streaming platforms. The prevalence of services like Spotify, Apple Music, and YouTube emphasizes the fact that all music is available anytime and anywhere. Gone are the days when young people treasured cassette and CD collections. The advent of streaming services has greatly increased music accessibility, likely fostering a diverse musical interest among younger generations.

Establishing a Healthy Student-Teacher Relationship

Because Gen Z and Gen Alpha students are open to exploring new types of music, there is considerable opportunity for teachers to introduce them to new styles and help shape their preferences in positive ways. To do this, it is essential for the teacher and student to build a relationship of trust, empathy, and communication. One model that instructors can consult for building this type of bond is *transformative pedagogy*.[23] This approach places emphasis on expanding a student's depth of understanding to facilitate ownership of knowledge and skill development. It promotes both performance and learning outcomes but emphasizes the process of learning. This pedagogical style is open and informative, prioritizing sense making and contextualizing content. It also highlights the necessity for the teacher to work closely with the student in every aspect of the learning process.[24] For instructors hoping to make their teaching more transformative, Gemma Carey and her colleagues posit they should focus on the following areas:

> **Purpose of Practice.** Refocus the intention of practicing so that consolidation and application are the goals rather than just trying to get it right.
>
> **Pedagogical Agility.** Experiment with new teaching methods and developing a versatile toolkit for various situations.
>
> **Approach to Diagnosis.** Encourage a collaborative approach between teacher and student to solve problems.
>
> **Approach to Meaning Making.** Discuss shared meanings in partnership with the student.[25]

To help build this collaborative approach, there are several things teachers can do. For example, instructors can rethink how they sequence effective modeling. Modeling needs to happen sandwiched between student reflection and inquiry. These cues from the student can guide the teacher, indicating when modeling will be helpful, and the teacher will be more effective because the student has already expressed a desire to understand and will be more receptive to deeper learning.

Teachers can also help to develop students' approach to feedback through questioning and steering them to greater specificity. It is important for instructors to acknowledge students' experiences and emotions by allowing time for these conversations. Transformative pedagogy helps promote self-direction, and facilitating this dynamic is more complex than just offering the balance between guidance and freedom.[26] When students have developed a strong sense of self-direction, they are more likely to embody self-efficacy and overall experience heightened motivation.

To continue building rapport with students, teachers may also want to investigate other approaches. Several researchers looked at the presence of vitality in music lessons, as this emotion is often a result of positive and healthy relationships. They observed that high-vitality lessons were characterized by the teacher and student mutually agreeing on goals and objectives at the beginning of the sessions. Establishing this structure provided a framework within which both parties could engage freely. Lessons that exhibited low vitality offered more choices for students with fewer goals and objectives. Furthermore, the teachers who asked the students more questions not only promoted critical thinking but also encouraged discussion so they could get to know the students more deeply.[27]

Nonverbal behavior can also have a major impact on the rapport between teacher and student. Teacher-immediacy behaviors refer to one's use of space, gaze, and touch. These actions can include leaning in, eye contact, shaking hands, high fives, and tone of voice. These positive behaviors are called "liking" behaviors. Teachers can be judged quite quickly based on their nonverbal behavior, so it is important for them to be aware of these aspects of communication to facilitate mutual respect with their students.

Good rapport in a lesson can be identified if there is more indication of specific progress, more laughter, and more sharing about the teacher's personal music history and the student's life beyond lessons. Proximity can also be an indication of a healthy, positive rapport. Successful teachers will always be aware of not letting any physical barriers separate them from making a connection with their students. Effective teachers will always express themselves visually and aurally.[28]

Exposing Students to Different Musical Styles

After teachers establish camaraderie with students, how can they leverage this advantage to increase their exposure to other musical styles and expand their musical preferences? Well, let us count the ways! First, it is crucial for teachers to take advantage of the fact that current young generations are open to all kinds of music. Therefore, their minds are already primed to explore new genres. Because of this, it is crucial to continually encourage them to explore various musical styles.

A suitable starting point for any teacher would be to get to know each student as early as possible and learn about their music preferences. If they feel comfortable doing so, they may be willing to share what is on their own streaming playlists. This will likely provide an idea of what they like to listen to for pleasure. For transfer students, it is common for teachers to ask about repertoire played in the past. Also, inviting them to reflect on what music they enjoyed playing as well as what challenges they faced will provide more insight into their preferences.

While developing an understanding of students' musical tastes, teachers can also begin the process of exposing them to different musical styles. Creating playlists collaboratively is a time-efficient way to encourage students to listen to a broad variety of pieces and songs. This is also something that young people are very comfortable doing and can serve as an opportunity for students to share knowledge with their teachers. If you are not familiar with making accounts on popular streaming platforms like Spotify and YouTube, then ask your students to help you out!

Playlists can be organized according to themes, and they can be arranged according to time. For example, perhaps you would like to rotate your students through different playlists each month or even each week so that they experience variety. Playlists can also be customized specifically for each student or a group of students. Include not just Western classical music but also works from around the world that underline unique harmonies, rhythms, and affects. Incorporate more popular genres by contemporary artists but also music from several decades ago, such as rock, disco, soul, and big band. Musical theater also has captivated the interests of the public. Immersing students in recorded performances will bolster their interest in attending live performances, as well. The more music students are exposed to, the more comfortable they will be playing those styles of music. This is especially important if students have not experienced a wide variety of music growing up.

The last step for helping to nurture students' musical awareness is to get them to participate so that they are playing or performing music from a vast array of styles. This active involvement will help them to appreciate the music even more.[29] Immersing oneself in a piece of music, exploring its intricacies, solving its challenging puzzles, and crafting an artistic interpretation enables individuals to truly grasp the essence of the style and appreciate its value. The structure of music lessons naturally supports this cycle of musical engagement, and it is beneficial for us to leverage this approach.

Notes

1. Alinka Greasley and Alexandra Lamont, "Musical Preferences," in *The Oxford Handbook of Music Psychology*, 2nd ed., ed. Susan Hallam, Ian Cross, and Michael H. Thaut, 263–82 (Oxford University Press, 2016), 268; Fei Jia and Emmanuel Koku, "Making American Friends: The Effects of Musical Tastes and English Proficiency on Chinese International Students' Social Networks in the United States," *Journal of Intercultural Communication Research* 48, no. 1 (2019): 6, https://doi.org/10.1080/17475759.2018.1549585.
2. Greasley and Lamont, "Musical Preferences," 277.
3. Rudolf E. Radocy and David J. Boyle, *Psychological Foundations of Music Behavior* (Charles C. Thomas, 2012), 404.
4. Greasley and Lamont, *Musical Preferences*, 268.
5. Christopher Andrews, Kate Gardiner, Tushar Kalpeshkumar Jain, Yalda Olomi, and Adrian C. North, "Culture, Personal Values, Personality, Uses of Music, and Musical Taste," *Psychology of Aesthetics, Creativity, and the Arts* 16, no. 3 (August 2022): 473, https://doi.org/10.1037/aca0000318.
6. Adrian North, "Individual Differences in Musical Taste," *American Journal of Psychology* 123, no. 2 (Summer 2010): 203–7, https://link.gale.com/apps/doc/A336671402/AONE?u=tall85761&sid=bookmark-AONE&xid=61075c4e.
7. Kevin Lewis, Marco Gonzalez, and Jason Kaufman, "Social Selection and Peer Influence in an Online Social Network," *Proceedings of the National Academy of Sciences of the United States of America* 109, no. 1 (January 3, 2012): 70, https://www.jstor.org/stable/23076233.
8. Jia and Koku, "Making American Friends," 14–15; Adam J. Lonsdale, "Musical Taste, In-Group Favoritism, and Social Identity Theory: Re-Testing the Predictions of the Self-Esteem Hypothesis," *Psychology of Music* 49, no. 4 (July 2021): 817–27, https://doi.org/10.1177/0305735619899158.
9. Josh H. McDermott, Alan F. Schultz, Eduardo A. Undurraga, and Ricardo A. Godoy, "Indifference to Dissonance in Native Amazonians Reveals Cultural Variation in Music Perception," *Nature* 535, no. 7613 (July 28, 2016): 547–50, https://doi.org/10.1038/nature18635.
10. Kevin Droe, "Music Preference and Music Education: A Review of Literature," *Update: Applications of Research in Music Education* 24, no. 2 (Spring–Summer 2006): 23–24, https://doi.org/10.1177/87551233060240020103.
11. Radocy and Boyle, *Psychological Foundations*, 420.
12. Ibid.
13. Droe, "Music Preference," 24.
14. Greasley and Lamont, "Musical Preferences," 269.
15. Radocy and Boyle, *Psychological Foundations*, 422.
16. Rudolf E. Radocy, "Effects of Authority Figure Biases on Changing Judgments of Musical Events," *Journal of Research in Music Education* 24, no. 3 (Fall 1976): 119–28, https://doi.org/10.2307/3345155.

17 Droe, "Music Preference," 24.
18 Christian Derbaix and Maud Derbaix, "Intergenerational Transmissions and Sharing of Musical Taste Practices," *Journal of Marketing Management* 35, nos. 17–18 (2019): 1602, https://doi.org/10.1080/0267257X.2019.1669691.
19 Sigrún Lilja Einarsdóttir, "'I Didn't Like Gilbert and Sullivan... Then I Found They Were Really Very Good'—'Learned Musical Taste' in the Context of an Amateur Choral Ensemble," *International Review of the Aesthetics and Sociology of Music* 51, no. 2 (December 2020): 215, https://www.jstor.org/stable/26959869.
20 Emily Hird and Adrian North, "The Relationship Between Uses of Music, Musical Taste, Age, and Life Goals," *Psychology of* Music 49, no. 4 (July 2021): 872–89, https://doi.org/10.1177/0305735620915247.
21 Lonsdale, "Musical Taste, In-Group Favoritism," 817–27.
22 David Crider, "Listening, but Not Being Heard: Young Women, Popular Music, Streaming, and Radio," *Popular Music and Society* 45, no. 5 (2022): 600–616, https://doi.org/10.1080/03007766.2022.2111513.
23 Gemma Marian Carey, Ruth Bridgstock, Peter Taylor, Erica McWilliam, and Catherine Grant, "Characterising One-to-One Conservatoire Teaching: Some Implications of a Quantitative Analysis," *Music Education Research* 15, no. 3 (2013): 361–62, https://doi.org/10.1080/14613808.2013.824954.
24 Leah Coutts, "Selecting Motivating Repertoire for Adult Piano Students: A Transformative Pedagogical Approach," *British Journal of Music Education* 35, no. 3 (November 2018): 287, https://doi.org/10.1017/S0265051718000074.
25 Carey et al., "Characterising One-to-One," 366.
26 Coutts, "Selecting Motivating Repertoire," 286.
27 Jennifer Blackwell, Peter Miksza, Paul Evans, and Gary E. McPherson, "Student Vitality, Teacher Engagement, and Rapport in Studio Music Instruction," *Frontiers in Psychology* 11 (May 2020): 1–12, https://doi.org/10.3389/fpsyg.2020.01007.
28 Christopher Johnson, Alice-Ann Darrow, and Becky J. A. Eason, "Novice and Skilled Music Teachers' Nonverbal Behaviors and Their Relationship to Perceived Effectiveness and Rapport," *Bulletin of the Council for Research in Music Education*, no. 178 (Fall 2008): 73–83, https://www.jstor.org/stable/40319340.
29 Einarsdóttir, "'I Didn't Like Gilbert,'" 216.

8 A Peek into the Studio of Today

To gain a better understanding of what independent piano instructors are doing in their studios today, we interviewed seven teachers. These conversations led to wide-ranging topics and offered us more insight into effective strategies in today's studio. With each teacher's permission, interviews were recorded, reviewed, and summarized in a narrative that each interviewee carefully checked and modified to ensure their story was expressed accurately. We hope you enjoy learning about these teachers' approaches as much as we did.

Penny Lazarus: Paving the Way for Project-Based Studios

In the span of ten years, Penny Lazarus has experienced a revolutionary yet organic change in her piano studio. She said, "If I were teaching today the way I taught ten years ago, I wouldn't have the success with these kids." Back then, she would have considered herself a primarily classical piano teacher who may have dabbled a little bit in some other genres. However, with the substantial social and political changes plus the worldwide medical crisis of COVID-19, Penny has found herself teaching a very different type of student these days.

Penny said that today's middle and high school students are very conscious and aware of the strife during the pandemic, and this has influenced their outlook on the world. As has been mentioned countless times before, these young people have a natural affinity for digital technology, which has trained them to consume a lot of content on their own. Because Penny has been willing to explore creative ways to motivate and engage her clientele, she has seen a 92 percent return rate in her studio of forty-five students. Those who leave at the end of a school year are graduating from high school or moving out of town with their families. Let's examine the key to Penny's success!

The cornerstone of Penny's transformation is the implementation of the project-based studio framework. Rooted in project-based learning, this approach inspires students to easily recognize how their piano studies can make a difference in the world. They discover that their work together as a team can make waves in their community.[1] Also, students are afforded autonomy or at least some level of choice in repertoire. The constant collaboration ensures the studio does not have a top-down attitude. At the start of each year, Penny chooses a theme based on a current issue or event that is relevant to her students and their local community. Studio members are made aware of the theme so that they can keep it in mind as they think about their repertoire selections. Penny no longer thinks about music in terms of genres or categories, like classical versus pop versus musical theater versus jazz. She also does not religiously consider leveling labels, such as elementary, intermediate, and so on. Repertoire is chosen based on its connection with the overall studio theme and whether it is well suited for the developing pianist.

Students often bring in repertoire that they have heard online and want to play. Penny has found that her current students have very wide-ranging musical tastes. Their musical preferences are not limited to just the current popular hits. They include selections from classic movies, video games, Disney films, top artists of the day, anime shows and movies, and classical music. In the past, Penny found it difficult to find appropriate arrangements of contemporary music that were fulfilling and motivating for students. However, highly skilled pedagogical-based arrangers like Lisa Donovan Lucas and Chrissy Ricker (Piano Pronto) are creating first-rate arrangements of modern music for students.

When a student says they want to play a certain piece or song, Penny is not necessarily always the one looking for the score. Her students often research their own sheet music, and through this process, she helps them to become independent, active, savvy, and informed consumers. In lessons, she provides guidance on how to analyze arrangements for the required hand span for a piece and whether the melodic line and chord structure are satisfying. Even if a particular arrangement does not meet all the necessary criteria, Penny works with the student to adapt the score so that it suits the individual.

Many young people enjoy watching anime (Japanese animation), and Joe Hisaishi is a composer synonymous with anime-related media. Pieces like "Merry-Go-Round of Life" and "One Summer Day" are inspired by Chopin-esque and impressionistic influences, making the connection to standard repertoire quite seamless. Studio Ghibli is one of the top Japanese animation studios that produces much of this globally popular music. Hal Leonard also has produced a piano collection featuring many selections. Furthermore, anime music has received even more appreciation through Hisaishi's collaboration with Deutsche Grammophon and the Royal Philharmonic Orchestra.

The third- to fifth-grade crowd is currently attracted to Taylor Swift songs, and Penny does not shy away from encouraging the Swifties! Because the chords in Taylor Swift's songs are usually easily identifiable for her students, Penny incorporates a theory lesson. She also helps them to see how the lyrics are meant to empower them.

Penny's chosen project themes are broad enough to encompass a wide variety of the students' chosen music. Recently, she partnered with a local chapter of the Audubon Society, an organization dedicated to conserving bird species and their habitats. The specific focus of the project was on light pollution and how that affects wildlife. It was titled "We Share One Sky," and the culminating performance was held in December, meaning any Christmas and holiday music relating to stars and light fit with the theme. Students made pinhole cameras, and astronomers were also present at the performance so that students could see constellations. One student really wanted to play Pink Floyd's "The Great Gig in the Sky." A decade ago, Penny would have said no to this proposition, but her approach has shifted. Because the song fit so well with the project theme, Penny now envisions new possibilities with student-chosen repertoire.

Another project her studio embarked on was titled "A River Runs Through Us." The Merrimack River passes through her town of Newburyport, Massachusetts, and different cultures have strong connections to this body of water, including the Hispanic and Indigenous communities. The Portuguese community also has strong ties to the fishing industry in this area, and there is a history of protests due to the severe working conditions at leather and cotton mills along this river. So music related to twentieth-century labor movements, like "Erie Barge Canal" (originally known as "Low Bridge, Everybody Down"), and music by Bob Dylan and John Denver were incorporated to explore the history of this theme. The program of music at the performance took the audience on a journey along the river.

Penny's current theme is "Bridges and Borders," and all music for that performance project comes from the twenty-three countries in North America. She is even using the theme as a chance to focus on analyzing musical bridges in theory analysis.

Even as Penny works to incorporate a project-based approach in her studio, she still works with leveled repertoire and the Royal Conservatory of Music Certificate program. The projects have simply given more purpose and meaning for her studio's activities and its members. Penny feels that for teachers interested in adopting a similar approach, it is important to be aware of and sensitive to the issues surrounding some of these topics as well as potential partner organizations. Because everyone is digitally connected, students are fully aware of current events. Teachers need to thoroughly learn and research the history of any chosen theme before presenting it to students. Penny is careful to steer clear of political implications and instead focuses on topics that encourage kindness and generosity to foster conscientious stewards of our interconnected and precious world. Penny's ultimate goal is to help students feel that the work they do is work for good.

Story Takeaways

- **Adopt a project-based framework.** Choose themes tied to current events or community issues to give lessons a unifying purpose. Use this theme to guide repertoire selection and inspire student-led performances or presentations.
- **Empower student choice.** Allow students to bring in music they're passionate about—from anime to pop to classical—and use their interests as a springboard for deeper musical and theoretical exploration.
- **Foster collaboration and autonomy.** Encourage students to research their own sheet music and analyze arrangements together. Teach them how to assess and adapt pieces to fit their skill level and artistic goals.
- **Integrate cross-disciplinary learning.** Connect music to broader topics, like science, history, or social justice. Partner with local organizations (e.g., environmental groups, cultural centers) to create meaningful, real-world connections.
- **Balance innovation with structure.** Continue using traditional tools, like leveled repertoire and certification programs, but let project themes and student interests drive the creative direction of your studio.

See Penny's website at https://www.pennylazaruspianostudio.com/the-studio for more information.

Leila Viss: Tapping into Technology and Combating Anxiety with Creativity

For a number of years now, Leila Viss's name has been synonymous with the use of technology in the piano-teaching world. As an independent pre-college piano instructor, she has used technology in her lessons to engage students for her entire career. She feels that the constant use of digital tools has heightened her teaching and has enabled her to stay up to date with her students. They themselves are not necessarily tech savvy, but they're used to technology. This mindset has kept Leila ahead of the times and has allowed her to develop and change with her students. She aptly noted that we have all changed, most notably mentioning that all of us have shorter attention spans as we have adapted to the world around us. Reduced focus is a trait often associated with younger generations—to the point where it can be a stereotype. Leila emphasized that it's important not to pass judgment on the youth. She contends that if we feel we are too different from them, then it means we just have not caught up with the times.

Leila is a classically trained pianist who uses her strong traditional training as a springboard for customizing her students' lessons. She commented that everything these days, from food and beverage to fashion, home decor, and technology are tailored to individual preferences, and music lessons are really no different. Students who have a choice (or at least feel like they have a choice) in what they study will more likely continue with their piano instruction. Leila also keeps students engaged by planning fast-paced lessons that involve numerous off-the-bench activities. As a general pedagogical approach, she is shifting more to hearing and feeling the music first before having the students play. Her teaching is now more influenced by whole body movement.

The advent of the iPad in 2010 was a game changer for Leila's use of technology in the piano studio, as it enhanced accessibility and convenience. When choosing apps and other technological tools to use, she uses three criteria: It must be (1) easy to use, (2) customizable, and (3) immediately beneficial and functional for the lesson. One app that has made a huge difference in motivating her students to continue their progress at home is *Practice Space*. This intuitive platform is essentially a digital assignment book, but Leila describes it as more than just an online notebook. It is more like a pipeline of information, where the teacher can communicate directly with the student throughout the week. Think of it as a weeklong texting conversation that may include some written tips, videos, backing tracks, and questions and answers. This type of ongoing communication is perhaps what modern-day young people are more used to.

The platform helps to foster a connection between student and teacher that transfers to the lesson in positive ways. Leila feels the use of this app does not significantly add to her workload. In fact, she is more efficient and organized. Students also send her short videos of their playing throughout the week, and as a result, she has a more accurate representation of each student's playing when they come to their lessons. That way, she can dive right into the aspects of their pianism that need attention. Not everyone in her studio writes her back on the platform and sends her videos, however she finds those who do really excel.

To help motivate students, Leila employs a number of strategies. She organizes challenges for her students and schedules them in little spurts. By giving them the choice of what they'll accomplish, she ensures they will have agency. Goals are characterized by being achievable and clear and having a specific time limit. Leila also feels it is very important that students are playing repertoire that they like and that fits their musical tastes.

This does not mean they are only exposed to a narrow selection of pieces. She often designs a unit for her studio where everyone studies a piece from a specific genre or era. At the time of our conversation, her students were focused on a baroque unit, and each student was working on a piece from that era. For those students who may not naturally be inclined to enjoy this repertoire, she told them it was a different type of music that would take a lot of discipline to learn. She would then proceed to help them find an appropriate piece they also enjoyed.

We ended our conversation with a profound topic. Many have noted that young people today seem more anxious. Leila agrees that anxiety is on the rise. She noted a higher level of anxiety among her students during the COVID-19 pandemic, but this has since dissipated. She commented on the challenges social media and video games pose and believes it boils down to the parents guiding their children in making appropriate choices. She feels fortunate that her students come from supportive families, resulting in minimal anxiety among them.

Leila's approach to addressing anxiety is inspiring. She referenced *Beyond Anxiety* by Dr. Martha Beck, highlighting that the opposite of anxiety is not calm but creativity. She stressed that the first step to enhancing creativity is curiosity and emphasized that all teachers should be curious. There are two types of curiosity: one driven by a sense of lack and the other by genuine interest. Leila and her family know firsthand how creativity can serve as a therapy for overcoming a traumatic experience. They chronicle their harrowing journey in the book *Found in the Wake: Rising from the Depths of a Devastating Boat Strike*, and through the development of this manuscript, they found peace, acceptance, and serenity. By being inquisitive and seeking new perspectives and solutions, creativity can pave the road for gaining new strength and resilience.

Story Takeaways

- **Integrate technology with purpose.** Use digital tools like iPads and apps that are easy to use, customizable, and immediately beneficial. These tools can enhance communication, track progress, and keep students engaged between lessons.
- **Design fast-paced, multisensory lessons.** Incorporate off-the-bench activities and whole-body movement to maintain focus and deepen musical understanding. Prioritize hearing and feeling music before playing to support kinesthetic and aural learning.
- **Offer personalized learning paths.** Tailor lessons to students' musical tastes while still exposing them to a broad range of styles and eras. Let students feel ownership by giving them choices in repertoire and learning goals.
- **Use short-term challenges to build motivation.** Create minigoals with clear, achievable outcomes and time limits. Let students choose their challenge focus to foster agency and commitment.
- **Combat anxiety through creativity and curiosity.** Encourage creative expression as a way to build resilience. Model curiosity as a teacher. Explore new tools, repertoire, and teaching strategies to stay inspired and connected with students.

For more information on Leila, visit her website at https://www.leilaviss.com/, and check out the page on her book at https://www.leilaviss.com/found-in-the-wake.

Chee-Hwa Tan: Solving Creative Conundrums

Chee-Hwa Tan is a well-established composer of pedagogical works in the United States. *A Child's Garden of Verses*, *Through the Window Pane*, and *Windy Nights and Other Tales* are among her works that are studied and performed by developing pianists across several countries. As mentioned in previous chapters, Gen Z and Gen Alpha students enjoy the process of creating, taking ownership of their work, and expressing themselves through music. In our conversation, we spoke about using creativity to motivate students in the piano studio.

Like the other practitioners interviewed for this book, Chee-Hwa's inspiration comes from her own private practice of teaching. She has recently taught a number of transfer high school students, many of whom were playing advanced repertoire. As she astutely observes, the majority of developing pianists do not enjoy working on technique. To help them make the connection between the physical and artistic aspects of playing, Chee-Hwa always starts talking about a specific technical skill by focusing on the emotion of the music and the student pianist's musical intentions. For example, she stated that for polyrhythms, rather than figuring out mathematically what a player needs to do, it's important to focus on the feeling of the polyrhythm and the tension inherently caused by the rhythms. Chee-Hwa emphasized that it's crucial for students to live within the discomfort of the polyrhythm for a while; it is through this experience that students will start to understand how the polyrhythm makes sense to them in their individual ways. As a result, they will envision the end goal, comprehend how the polyrhythm makes them feel, and then finally focus on communicating that feeling to listeners.

Recently, Chee-Hwa has turned this approach into a step-by-step process that all teachers can use. She has updated her *Once upon a Journey* and *A Child's Garden of Verses* with prompts that help students and their instructors connect emotions to specific technical challenges. The activities encourage students to process emotion through art, word, or movement before learning technique at the piano.

One example is the piece "As Eagles Soar," which focuses on reinforcing arpeggio technique. Prior to identifying the physical motion needed to play this piece successfully, the teacher and student can discuss why composers may choose to use arpeggios in their music. In this piece, arpeggios create the sense of soaring. Chee-Hwa then points to scientific fact that for eagles to truly soar, they cannot use only their own strength; they must use the wind current to help propel them. This translates to the theme of interdependence and normalizing asking for help. She then provides questions encouraging students to engage in mindful reflection about the intended emotion so that their attention is less focused on the mechanics of playing the arpeggios. The final step leads students to transferring the envisioned emotion to the piano so that the artistic vision can guide and inspire the technical solution.

Chee-Hwa is a firm believer in "preparing the emotions" associated with repertoire before diving in and learning how to play any given piece. She mentioned that these early steps take time, perhaps even a few weeks or months. Remember, this repertoire is meant to reinforce technical skills. However, once the students make it to the point where they are playing the technique feat, they can truly transfer what they learned in the first steps about emotion and achieve success. Gen Z and Gen Alpha students tend to be more attuned to emotions, making emotional connection feel like a natural and welcome part of their learning experience.

Story Takeaways

- **Lead with emotion, not mechanics.** Begin technical instruction by exploring the emotional intent behind the music. Help students connect with how a piece should feel before addressing how it should be played.
- **Use storytelling and imagery to teach technique.** Frame technical challenges (like arpeggios or polyrhythms) through metaphors and narratives. For example, relate arpeggios to the soaring of an eagle to inspire fluid motion and emotional expression.
- **Incorporate multimodal creativity.** Before students touch the piano, invite them to express the emotion of a piece through drawing, writing, or movement. This primes their imagination and deepens their connection to the music.
- **Normalize discomfort as part of growth.** Encourage students to live in the discomfort of complex techniques like polyrhythms. Emphasize that emotional understanding can guide them through technical challenges.
- **Prepare emotion before technique.** Use reflective prompts and discussions to help students internalize the emotional landscape of a piece. Let this emotional preparation guide their technical development over time.

For more information on Chee-Hwa, visit her at https://dayungsampanmusic.com/.

Marie Lee: Finding Strength in Numbers

Marie Lee of Nevada has harnessed the power of the group dynamic and runs a studio where she exclusively teaches group classes. It all started because of a long wait list for individual lessons—she had so many students hoping to study with her because there was a piano-teacher shortage in her city, Las Vegas. She wanted to keep all of her students but didn't have room in her schedule to accommodate them.

Marie started learning about the Mayron Cole Group Piano method and discovered ways to sequence piano-learning concepts that would be suitable for groups. At first, she had to do a lot of upselling to parents to convince them learning would take place in this setting. They were skeptical about whether their children could absorb knowledge just as well with other children in the room. Nevertheless, Marie persevered, and as she gained more confidence and experience teaching in this setting, both students and parents were hooked.

The one-to-one setting is the lesson environment most associated with piano instruction. The idea of one student receiving the complete attention of the teacher sitting nearby is synonymous with piano lessons. Among the many advantages of this approach, the most prominent is the ability to customize lessons and curriculum based on the student's needs. Many people may believe this is the sole or most effective method to teach piano, however there is an alternative. Group lessons, where two or more students work with one teacher at the same time, has been gaining traction for several decades, particularly in the United States.

The group piano-class setting is often associated with college-level curriculum. Music majors whose instruments are something other than piano often find themselves in a lab with multiple keyboards and headsets, learning how to play the instrument alongside a number of their peers. In recent years, this has extended to elementary, middle, and high schools across the country, offering more children access to piano instruction. Group piano as part of an independent teacher's studio is less common. However, this trend is changing.

Marie explained how her focus on group teaching has evolved over the years, as she now places significant emphasis on building community. She was inspired by her daughter's experience in an Irish step-dancing troupe, where her daughter loved working with the fellow dancers on her team, competing together, and building lifelong friendships in the process. Because their success relied on all members doing their part, they were highly motivated to work hard and make a meaningful contribution to the group. This sparked an idea in Marie's mind—she wanted her students to have the same experience.

As a result, Marie's group classes became piano teams that meet on a weekly basis to develop their individual skills as pianists and to work on group activities and repertoire. They prepare for about four to six performance opportunities each year, including a play-a-thon at the local mall and an event at a retirement home or assisted-living facility. Their more high-stakes events are festivals, with their biggest event being the National Federation Ensemble festival. Marie described how the students really look forward to these performance opportunities and value being a member of the team. They want to make sure they contribute to the group's success, and it highly motivates them to practice between group classes. This healthy type of social pressure is likely why young people are excited to be on sports teams—the opportunity to work as part of a group and see their friends motivates them to heighten their skills and show up to practice each week.

Another way Marie motivates her students is by hiring them as team mentors once they have taken lessons for a few years and have experience. Age is not a factor, as she once hired one of her ten-year-old students! Mentors have achieved a certain level of musical and pianistic skills and have the maturity to deal with responsibilities, like some administration work and even tutoring younger students. The mentors enjoy having the responsibilities, and it helps Marie with retaining students who may be at an age when they are prone to dropping out: They want a job, so they know they need to keep up with their piano skills to maintain this type of employment. Through their tutoring, mentors learn how to communicate with others. It can also serve as great motivation to practice. Marie has had some serious conversations with student mentors whose "practice didn't reflect their status." Upon realizing that their lack of effort did not reflect well on their mentor roles, they understood that a change in their personal practice was necessary to continue as mentors, making them aware of the consequences of their actions.

Marie has found that this intentional development of a community atmosphere has been successful in retaining students. Because they are part of an energetic and successful piano team, they want to stay in the group and continue with lessons. During and after the COVID-19 pandemic, many parents in her area switched to homeschooling. This caused them to seek out opportunities to enhance social interaction for their children. In some cases, this was their main priority when signing up for group piano lessons.

To ensure that students can stay on top of their practice assignments, Marie uses the app *Practice Space*, a platform that she started using during the pandemic. This enables her to easily create video tutorials, particularly when she wants to adopt a flipped-class format. Students are expected to learn things on their own at home and be prepared for the activities in class. Because they are all working as a team, there is a certain level of peer pressure spurring them on to practice accordingly at home.

One of Marie's current priorities involves equipping parents with the knowledge and awareness necessary to support successful music learning. She highlights that patience and kindness are essential for a teacher to be effective in this area. The key is to get to know and understand the parents' perspectives. Marie has found that she needs to be more intentional about explaining their role at home to help their children be successful. She focuses much of her communication on teaching parents about the importance of grit and helping them understand how long it can take to acquire new skills. Marie has also observed that especially after the pandemic, students, particularly those around the ages of thirteen to sixteen, had a more difficult time speaking with each other. She makes a conscious effort to break the ice in group class each week with these students.

Marie is clear that the group setting might not be the best fit for every child, and she is open about this with parents during the initial interview. It also might not be the best fit for every teacher, particularly because a studio like this involves multiple instruments as an upfront expense. Marie teaches out of a music store that custom-built a studio for her and acquired eight keyboards for her classroom. It is a unique and fortunate arrangement.

However, Marie wants teachers to know they don't have to be all in for group teaching: You don't have to go her route and exclusively teach in the group setting. She suggests that it can be helpful to include some type of group element as a part of studio offerings. For those thinking of converting to a fully group-class studio, she recommends finding a hired coach and networking with other group teachers. Attending the Music Teachers National Association's (MTNA) conference; the National Conference on Keyboard Pedagogy; or GroupIlluminatED, the virtual conference that Marie cochairs with Leila Viss, offers teachers a multitude of chances to interact with other experts.

In our discussion, Marie stated that most of her students do not intend to pursue a career in music. However, that does not mean she waters down her approach. It means that she must reset her expectations and educate her students' parents on how to do the same. Even with the limited time students have for daily practice and the fact that more parents are working and cannot supervise their child's practice regularly, Marie's goal is to foster the skill of music making. She wants to ensure that her students will return to the piano throughout their lives as an outlet for creativity, expression, and entertainment. Through their classes, she teaches such life skills as persistence, focus, fortitude, and empathy. Marie likes to remind her students that the world needs "good people playing good music." Through their piano playing, they can provide something others might not have and cultivate joy in people's lives.

Story Takeaways

- **Build a team-based studio culture.** Reframe group classes as "piano teams" to foster camaraderie, accountability, and motivation. Plan regular group performances and community events to give students shared goals and a sense of purpose.
- **Empower students through mentorship.** Create leadership roles for experienced students by hiring them as team mentors. This builds responsibility, reinforces their skills, and helps retain older students who might otherwise drop out.
- **Engage parents as partners.** Educate parents about the learning process, emphasizing patience, grit, and long-term growth. Be intentional about explaining their role in supporting practice and progress at home.
- **Create a welcoming social environment.** Prioritize community building, especially for students who may struggle with social interaction. Use icebreakers and team activities to help students connect and feel comfortable.

See Marie's website at https://www.musicalityschools.com/ for more information.

Joe Harkins: A Truly Customized Approach

Joe Harkins is an innovative and creative teacher who makes significant efforts to truly customize lessons according to his students' needs. While he may use a number of approaches, the center of all his thinking boils down to the music. He is very cognizant of the fact that young people are constantly surrounded by music, and they pick up tunes that are attractive to them as they encounter them in daily life. Perhaps it's a small motive from a TV series, video game, or movie or maybe something they heard their parents listen to. Whatever it may be, Joe's central pedagogical philosophy is that it is his job to incorporate that student's musical interests into their studies and make it work in a way that is meaningful to the student. He places emphasis on how students can enjoy music throughout their lifetimes.

As a musician with a background that is equally strong in classical and jazz training, Joe feels very comfortable arranging melodies and music clips his students enjoy and bring to him. He ensures that the arrangements are custom-crafted for individual students, making them both satisfying and appropriate to play at the piano. He recounted that he once had a six-year-old student who broke his left arm and could only play with his right arm. (Pianists know there is a lot of repertoire written solely for the left arm but not the right arm!) The student loved jazz music, so Joe arranged the melody of Duke Ellington's "Satin Doll" for him so that the student had something to play that he would enjoy. From a pedagogical perspective it was perfect: The song mainly consists of intervals of seconds, so the student was able to focus on perfecting his two-note slur articulation.

Joe has also noticed an increased interest in video game music. Sometimes he can find scores online, as publishers have also noted this interest with piano students. For example, Hal Leonard has published two levels of arrangements from the game *Minecraft*. Other times, his students may know certain melodies very well and can learn how to play them by rote. Finally, Joe may have to transcribe the music himself, and if this happens, it turns into a listening activity, as he works collaboratively with the student in the lesson. The most important factor is that all students are playing something that resonates with their individual preferences.

In contrast with students he has taught in the past, Joe has had to adapt his teaching strategies so that he remains relevant with his current students. He finds that technology is now used in very different ways and is such an integral part of daily life. For example, he encourages the use of the app *Chordie* in his studio lessons. This digital tool shows the notation as well as which keys to play on the piano.

These types of apps and YouTube tutorials (where the keys light up) have often been chastised by piano teachers, as they feel students could latch on to them and avoid learning how to read notation. Joe has a different perspective. Because the students are going to use them anyway, he embraces the technology and uses it to enhance their rote learning. It's an excellent example of meeting students where they are and guiding them toward proper use of a digital tool.

Joe has also noticed that students are used to fast-paced activity. He always makes sure that he has many activities planned for a lesson so that students avoid losing focus. Sometimes he puts on a three-minute timer so that he can motivate a student to focus on mastering one passage. Once the three minutes is up, they do another activity, usually away from the piano. One of these activities is a rhythm tree, which has a space elsewhere in the studio. Students choose a pop song they enjoy and a rhythmic value, and they tap along with the song. It's a simple but effective way to reset their focus while still incorporating a musical skill in the activity. Another important aspect of his pedagogical approach is increasing the students' awareness of topography. He has created the book series Piano Topography: Mapping the Keyboard to help pianists truly understand the visual and tactile aspects of musical patterns on the keys.

Joe also creates audio journals with his students. For this segment of the lesson, students choose something small to record that they can share with their parents later. One student played a chord progression as the backdrop to an informercial-type narrative he verbalized. It was a creative application of a necessary piano skill. Joe explained that this activity is particularly effective for students in method books who may not be at the level to play standard repertoire. Because their pieces may be much shorter and less complicated, creating these little recordings helps to make the practice of performing more permanent in their minds. He has also found that the way he formulates requests can make a significant difference in the student's mindset. For example, instead of asking a student to just play a review piece, he may say, "Give me a concert today!" and suddenly the student's outlook is transformed.

Developing a personal understanding of each student is important to Joe. He finds that his students bring random items to their lessons, including toys, pets, and even sports equipment. They often want to show him something from their lives at home. Rather than just smiling sweetly and saying, "That's nice," Joe always finds a way to incorporate that item into the lesson. His students may not have as many outlets to share things with others (perhaps a side effect of the pandemic), and the one-on-one interaction they receive at their lessons is crucial to their social well-being. In this way, he learns more about them as people and creates a lasting connection with each student.

To heighten student motivation to practice, there are a number of tried-and-true strategies Joe has come to rely on. First and foremost, giving students choice, or at least an illusion of choice, goes a long way in encouraging students to practice. He ensures that all the problem-solving and practice to create change takes place in the actual lesson so that students leave their lessons able to play their assignments. At-home practice simply reinforces what was learned in the lesson. Parents are aware their children can play their assignments, which helps them realize if something is amiss with at-home practice. Joe works with the parents behind the scenes and strategizes their involvement.

When prompted to offer advice for other teachers working with today's young generation, he humbly stated, "Don't take yourself too seriously." Often, as teachers, we can get wrapped up in our preparation, ways of thinking, and complex strategies. However, sometimes this can happen at the expense of a student-centered approach. Joe remarked that it is crucial to view "problem students" or problems with students as opportunities for instructors to grow as pedagogues. He reiterated that every child is a gift and that their lesson is precious time, as the teacher can make such an impact during their one-to-one interaction. No two lessons will be the same, and it's important to acknowledge and celebrate that type of unpredictability shaping our profession. Joe emphasized that the students should always come first and teachers should always ask themselves if their students leave lessons happier and changed from when they arrive.

Story Takeaways

- **Center lessons around student interests.** Use music students already love—from video games to jazz—to create custom arrangements that are both pedagogically sound and personally meaningful.
- **Embrace technology to aid rote learning.** Incorporate apps like *Chordie* and YouTube tutorials to support rote learning and visual engagement, guiding students in how to use these tools effectively.
- **Keep lessons dynamic and varied.** Use timers, off-bench activities, and creative tools like rhythm trees or audio journals to maintain focus and reinforce musical concepts in fun, memorable ways.
- **Foster personal connection.** Welcome students' personal stories and items into the lesson to build trust and deepen engagement. Use these moments to create meaningful musical connections.

- **Prioritize in-lesson success.** Ensure students can play their assignments before they leave the lesson. This builds confidence and makes home practice more effective and parent supported.

For more about Joe's studio, see https://www.harkinspianostudio.com/about, and for his book series, see https://www.harkinspianostudio.com/books.

Pilar Plazas: Moving to the Music

As a teacher who completed coursework at the Orff Institute in Salzburg, Austria, Pilar is committed to offering her students a multisensory approach in her piano lessons. The use of movement is now central to her pedagogical philosophy. In her early years as an instructor, Pilar said she used to just verbalize her instructions and would only speak about concepts. Soon, she realized she was taking advantage of just one tool out of all the other strategies available to her. She has found great success in engaging today's generation of young students by planning many different types of activities for their lessons and getting them off the bench. This has given her the opportunity to create different ways to emphasize the topic she is focusing on and involve their other senses.

To capture the attention of Generation Z and especially Generation Alpha students, Pilar employs a methodical approach to incorporate movement into piano lessons. She prepares all pianistic skills with movement by first having students dance and move freely to the music. Sometimes, they may even roll on the floor or swing ribbons through the air. Upper-body movement is also important. Because students are often glued to digital screens at school and at home, piano lessons can serve as an outlet for them to get up and move. Pilar noted that as students get older, they become more self-conscious about movement, so she adjusts her expectations accordingly. This is particularly true for students who start piano at an older age.

When working with young students, Pilar prioritizes clear, direct instruction over open-ended requests. Rather than asking, "Can you keep your feet flat on the floor?" she states, "Keep your feet flat on the floor." To make these directions more engaging, she often weaves them into imaginative stories that capture children's attention and make learning more enjoyable.

Pilar teaches young children in one-to-one lessons and group piano classes that have two or three students. She recommends one of these two formats to parents based on their child's learning needs and strengths. In the group setting, she finds that children sometimes take advice better from their peers and learn more from each other. For example, if one child is uncertain but sees another playing more confidently, she allows the interaction between the two students to occur naturally, letting one teach the other.

Pilar also encourages creativity through storybook reading. Every week the children each take a different storybook home to read. They return the following week, choose their favorite images from the book, and use those pictures to inspire a composition. Through these types of activities, the students explore the use of their own voice. Practice sheets for homework assignments keep the students accountable, such as indicating when they practiced (e.g., after brushing teeth in the morning or before bedtime). The children are eager to share their practice accomplishments, and they motivate each other. Student-led segments of the class encourage leadership development and confidence among the children.

Over the years, Pilar has gained a wide breadth of experience teaching in Colombia, Australia, and now the United States. As a result, she has identified some essential teaching strategies that work with the majority of students. Taking the time to get to know each student and make a connection with them is crucial for building trust. Once enough trust is built, the teacher can accurately determine how to pace different skills and prepare for certain goals. Like many teachers, Pilar concurs that it is important to adjust expectations depending on student needs. It is also crucial to identify which experiences bring joy to the individual students and then plan and create activities that will be meaningful to them. Allowing space and time for creativity and exploration is essential, especially because today's Generation Z and Alpha students are often intent on finding their own voice.

Story Takeaways

- **Incorporate movement to teach musical concepts.** Use dancing, ribbon play, and upper-body movement to prepare pianistic skills and engage students physically and musically.
- **Use clear, direct instructions.** Give specific, confident directions (e.g., "Keep feet flat on the floor"), and enhance them with imaginative storytelling to guide young learners.

- **Foster creativity through storytelling.** Have students read storybooks, choose favorite images, and use them as inspiration for weekly compositions to nurture self-expression.
- **Leverage peer learning in small groups.** Use group settings to encourage natural peer teaching and collaborative learning, especially effective for young children.
- **Personalize learning.** Take time to understand each student's personality and joy triggers, and tailor pacing and activities to match their individual needs and interests.

For more information, see Pilar's website at https://pndmusiceducation.com/.

Ashley Danyew: Striving for a Balanced Approach

As an independent teacher in Rochester, New York, with a large studio, Ashley Danyew has recently found herself teaching two distinct groups of students: slightly older teenagers who are clearly Generation Z and younger children who represent Generation Alpha. This situation has enabled her to notice some differences between the generations, causing her to reflect on their needs, challenges, and goals in intentional ways.

She first noted that a balanced repertoire plan is essential for any student. However, with Generation Z students, it is even more necessary. In congruence with some of the research referred to in earlier chapters, Ashley has noticed that individuals from Generation Z love listening to music from different time periods. They are not focused just on what is popular now. As a result, their diverse tastes offer lots of opportunities for the teacher when choosing their repertoire.

Ashley makes a point to follow up with music that is interesting to them. Rather than just dismiss a piece they may bring in and tell them to work on it at home on their own, Ashley includes it on their assignment sheet to "make it official." She explores YouTube videos with them, expanding their exposure to new styles and encouraging thoughtful listening to different performances. Other activities she has found engaging with these students include rewriting endings to pieces, having them role-play as the teacher to exercise their critical-thinking skills, and engaging in theoretical analysis.

Ashley is thrilled to see these students' curiosity about the mechanics of music and is eager to nurture their inquisitiveness. She has found that the Gen Z students she has worked with have perfectionist tendencies, and she needs to remind them that the process of learning is just as important as the final product.

With Generation Alpha students, Ashley has found that she is more intentional with planning. Lessons need to be quick paced, so in a typical forty-five-minute lesson, she aims to include nine different segments. She ensures that she mixes and matches activities regularly so that her Gen Alpha students are not doing too much of the same thing for too long.

She does more to balance their time on and off the bench, as they do need to be more active. Sometimes, to train the listening muscle, she plays their repertoire as they move freely around the room. After this listening-and-movement activity, Ashley may ask students to reflect or comment on something they heard. She always finds that their responses are more thoughtful, and they are more focused when they are moving while listening. It is an intentionally low-tech approach. Because that's not what the students are often accustomed to, it gives them a new experience.

Ashley's studio offerings include small-group gatherings to foster welcoming and less-intimidating performance settings. A special performance opportunity that all students engage in is an informance. This term was coined by Mary Pautz, who defines it simply as show-and-tell time. The purpose of an informance is to demonstrate to parents and other attendees what goes on in a music class rather than presenting a polished product.[2] Ashley's studio's informances usually involve five to six students, so the gathering is more intimate. In conjunction with the performances of their pieces, students also speak about their repertoire.

Ashley spoke about the different themes she has incorporated into recent informances. One theme focused on female composers. Students chose their repertoire based on selections Ashley had deemed appropriate for each student. All the repertoire chosen were by living composers, and Ashley had the idea to contact the composers directly. She had students select questions for each composer, and together they created letters that Ashley then emailed. Some of the questions by the older and more-advanced students focused on the compositions. However, the questions from the younger children often focused on personal preferences, like favorite color.

They received a 100 percent response rate, and the students were thrilled to read their printed letters that were emailed back to Ashley.

At the informance, students spoke about the letters they received and provided the audience with more personal insight regarding the composers of their repertoire. A theme from 2024 focused on the total solar eclipse that captivated many people across North America. At this informance, students played repertoire related to outer space and engaged in activities with the audience. These activities often came from their own lessons and offered students the opportunity to take on leadership roles.

Ashley also schedules about six to eight studio classes per school year. She limits the class size to three to four students so that they can really interact and get to know each other. After every class, she emails a written summary of the studio class to parents so that they are aware of all the things their children have accomplished.

Another interesting observation that Ashley made was the role of parents. She has found that the millennial parents of Gen Z and Gen Alpha students seem to be more overwhelmed, and ongoing communication can sometimes be difficult. She has found that they tend to be less connected to their children's musical study and may expect them to practice independently and be self-motivated. This was also expressed by other teachers we interviewed.

To effectively motivate students to practice regularly, Ashley has found it is crucial that students set realistic practice expectations. There's no use in saying one will practice seven days a week when it never happens. She has encouraged her students to set practice reminders on their phones. Ashley also incorporates YOYO (You're on Your Own) pieces—an idea from Marvin Blickenstaff. These are often pieces that a student has expressed interest in learning. Ashley helps them get started with learning a piece in their lesson, and then the student has to figure out the rest at home. The independence can be highly enticing for the student.

When asked to provide advice for other teachers, Ashley stated that it's important to go with your intuition and to individualize lessons. She has found it crucial to help students make connections with other activities they engage in throughout the week. Recently she had one student who was negotiating left-hand octave jumps in one of her pieces. This same student was also involved in aerial arts. Once they identified the relationship between the left-hand jumps and aerial arts, the technical challenge suddenly seemed surmountable for the student. Ashley reemphasized that the teaching studio is akin to a teaching lab—it's important to experiment and try new ideas with students on a regular basis. Through this process of trial and error, teachers will have access to all kinds of pedagogical innovation.

Story Takeaways

- **Differentiate by generation.** Tailor lesson pacing and structure to suit Gen Z's reflective curiosity and Gen Alpha's need for variety and movement-based learning.
- **Balance repertoire with student choice.** Include student-selected pieces in official assignments, and explore them together to validate their interests and deepen engagement.
- **Use informances to build confidence.** Host informal, small-group performances where students share both their music and personal insights, fostering communication and ownership.
- **Encourage independence with YOYO pieces.** Assign "You're on Your Own" pieces to promote self-directed learning and build confidence in independent practice.
- **Connect music to life.** Help students relate musical challenges to other activities they enjoy, reinforcing learning through personal connections and real-world analogies.

For more about Ashley, see her website at https://www.ashleydanyew.com/.

Notes

1 Fey Cole, *An Educator's Guide to Project-Based Learning: Turning Theory into Practice* (David Fulton, 2024).

2 Mary Pautz, "Both Performance and Informance: Not 'Either—Or' in Elementary General Music," *General Music Today* 23, no. 3 (April 2010): 20–26, https://doi.org/10.1177/1048371309361182.

9 Proven Strategies You Can Use

Throughout this book, we highlight the characteristics of Generations Z and Alpha students, identify the challenges they face, address how to foster creativity, and consider how we can ascertain and celebrate their musical tastes. We also stepped into the piano studios of independent teachers around the United States to get a sense of what has worked for them. Now is the time to reflect and consider what works for you!

In this chapter, we compile the strategies and resources discussed throughout this book as well as additional approaches and instructional tools you may find useful when working with today's students. We organize this chapter as a practical reference list, allowing you to quickly locate effective solutions. The strategies are categorized into three main themes that we feel form the cornerstone of impactful teaching:

1. **Motivating Your Students:** Spark excitement and intrigue for students.
2. **Customizing Lessons for Your Students:** Communicate in the individual student's language based on their own preferences.
3. **Inspiring Students to Engage in True Self-Expression:** Facilitate deeper thinking and creativity.

Many effective strategies naturally embody elements of all three themes, which is covered in the final section of this chapter, "Multimodal Activities." This framework streamlines navigation, providing clarity and ease of reference.

Motivating Your Students

Collaboration

With heightened globalization, our world is interconnected. We rely on each other to progress and move forward. When we work as a team, our drive to succeed is motivated by our desire to contribute and be of value to the group. Marie expressly communicated the magic of teamwork. So many young people's activities are in teams, where they are in community with each other: sports, youth groups, clubs, gaming, and social media. If we don't harness the power of collaboration in piano playing, it will not seem as appealing.

Music Ensembles

The traditional way of fostering collaboration in the piano studio is by getting students to play duets. While this is a great way to start, it's not the only option we have at our fingertips. Developing collaborative skills in real time at the same instrument is crucial for any developing pianist. However, sometimes students and parents may complain about finding room in their schedules to get together for rehearsals.

In this case, a digital collaboration (like the ones we learned to do during the COVID-19 pandemic) might help students to reap the benefits of ensemble work. Each student can learn and rehearse their own parts individually, communicate remotely to discuss musical intentions, record parts individually, and then again collaborate remotely to create the digital ensemble. Furthermore, the inclusion of technology in this project can be enticing for many students. Teachers can also work with groups of students to create their own arrangements. This is discussed further in the "Inspiring Students to Engage in True Self-Expression" section.

Tools and Resources for Digital Collaborations

Canva: A popular graphic-design platform, Canva is also a convenient tool with which to create short videos. Multiple videos can be posted on one page and manually synced to create one fluid ensemble performance. Just make sure that everyone is playing at the same beats per minute (BPM)! This may be accomplished with a click track, which can include a metronome click paired with instructions or harmonies to guide students as they play. Textbox 9.1 is an example of a Canva-made virtual ensemble.

Openshot and Shotcut Video-Editing Platforms: Both Openshot and Shotcut are open-source video software that are downloadable for Windows, Mac, and Linux. Create a click track or simply an agreed-upon BPM played on a metronome that students can play in headphones while recording their parts.

> **Textbox 9.1 "That What's Friends Are For" by Burt Bacharach and Carole Bayer Sager, Group Piano Ensemble Arrangement**
>
> Group Piano Program, Florida State University, College of Music, Spring 2024, https://youtu.be/LBYEywL7si0?si=6XZYUmzwxkmqZytg.

Open Broadcaster Software: Commonly known as OBS, this free and open-source program is widely used for live streaming and video recording. It allows users to combine multiple sources (e.g., multiple cameras, images, text) into customizable configurations or scenes that can be easily switched during a broadcast or recording. It includes an audio mixer and with some exploration is quite user friendly.

Project-Based Studio Activities

Penny vividly described how a project-based studio has assisted her with transforming her teaching so that she is able to fully engage her students. Choosing a theme that connects closely with the local community can be a great way for students to see the results of their action up close. For example, creating a program of music that connects with a nature reserve, body of water, or museum in the area may even attract audience members from the wider community to your studio recital. In this type of activity, the performance project does not feel complete without each person's contribution and the group works toward a common mission of bringing awareness to a specific cause.

Penny also talked about how sometimes she has organized practice marathons for her students. Students find a sponsor (often their own parents), and they raise money based on the amount they practice. Sponsorship rates average around five to twenty cents per hour, something that is still affordable. As a team, the studio picked a charity to support with their raised donations.

Choosing a theme can sometimes feel like a challenge. Also, it may be important to skirt around some divisive topics to maintain studio harmony. Here are some ideas to get the project theme juices flowing:

- Students choose a piece of art or exhibit from a local museum and a repertoire inspired by it.

- In communities that have diverse populations, students can play music representing the different cultures.
- The studio can collaborate on group research to learn about the local history of a body of water or natural attractions in the area and then choose repertoire inspired by that history.

Figure 9.1 shows all the possibilities that can stem from this type of project, focusing on Wakulla Springs, one of the world's largest and deepest freshwater springs, located near Tallahassee, Florida.

Even this short brainstorm reveals how diverse and expansive the program's repertoire can be. Each studio member will be able to find something that relates to them. Classical and popular music along with new compositions can be easily integrated into this theme. Furthermore, if one can't find the music from the original *Tarzan* films, a quick jump to the animated Disney movie can offer alternatives. Repertoire by underrepresented Native American and Spanish composers can also be incorporated, and there are many pedagogical works written that depict some of these animals. With a narration of Wakulla Spring's history and vivid photos, a program of music based on this local gem

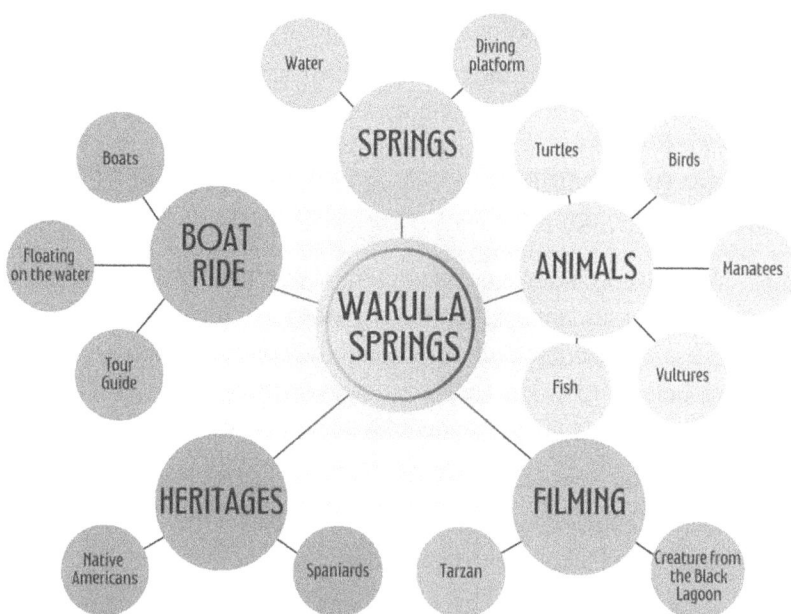

Figure 9.1 Concept map of topics based on Wakulla Springs. *Illustration by the author.*

will excite students to contribute to this group effort and learn a bit more about their local community.

Resources for Project-Based Studios

Aileen's Music Room (https://aileensmusicroom.com/2019/12/42-project-based-learning-in-the-music-room/): This page offers definitions, ideas, and further resources for project-based activities in the studio.

Smithsonian Learning Lab (https://learninglab.si.edu/): This free and interactive platform offers access to resources from across the Smithsonian museums. Educators can create customized collections to assist with project-based and interdisciplinary projects they are working on with their students in the studio.

The Curious Piano Teachers (https://thecuriouspianoteachers.org/): This global community offers a library of teaching resources and videos that encourage student-centered learning and cross-curricular inquiry. A paid subscription is required. This resource can be helpful for teachers wanting to integrate storytelling, movement, and cultural exploration in their lessons.

Informances

Having students verbalize and explain what they are playing helps us as teachers ensure they have gained a deep understanding of their repertoire. When students have greater insight about their music, they will be more motivated to practice it. Add the layer of collaboration on top of that, and students will be eager to participate. In her story, Ashley explained how informances can be laid-back events where only a small group of students and their parents are present. Once students gain comfort with this format, these workshop-type programs can be taken on the road to places like seniors' homes, schools, and libraries. Once again, integration with the wider community can be an essential motivator for students who are thirsty for social interaction.

Games

We talked about the art of play and how games have long been used by educators. Here are some activities and resources geared specifically for piano instruction that have been proven to increase motivation.

Floor Staff

There are many possibilities for games with a floor staff! You can either make one with duct tape and construction paper, buy a cloth floor staff online, or create one with shoelaces directly on the floor. Students can be challenged to step on certain notes, intervals, or chords or throw beanbags on the staff to gamify the naming of notes. Groups of students can also compete with two floor staves to see who can make the most chords or find the most notes the fastest!

Music Trivia

Set up a *Jeopardy!*-style game for groups or create your own type of trivia format and ask students various questions about music history, music theory, ear training, and anything else you would like to include. *Jeopardy!* templates, such as the one found at https://jeopardylabs.com/, make it easy to create your own game in minutes.

Note-Word-Spelling Competitions

Printing out individual note flash cards (cardstock or laminating ensure more durability) can provide an assortment of games to try with groups of students and in one-to-one lessons. Try calling out different words that can be spelled with letters of the musical alphabet (e.g., *decaf*, *cabbage*, *facade*), and use it as a timed activity in one-to-one lessons or as a competition in a group setting. The cards can also be used for traditional note drills. Joy Morin of the *Color in My Piano* blog created an attractive set of note cards you can print and cut out to use with your students (https://colorinmypiano.com/tag/flashcards/).

Music Bingo

While some students may not have a history of knowing how to play bingo, they will easily learn when you introduce this game, customized for music concepts! While this example from Teachers Pay Teachers (https://www.teacherspayteachers.com/Product/Music-BINGO-Notes-Symbols-and-Terms-1608842) is focused on music terms and symbols, the website also features an array of music bingo versions including rhythms, notes, and melodic dictation.

Rhythm-Dictation Games

Rhythm is the foundation of all musical structure, so it is worth spending time heightening our students' awareness of this important element. Joy Morin of the *Color in My Piano* blog once again provides great resources. Students can play a trick-or-treat game, where they draw either a "treat" card or a "trick" card from a pile that directs the student to clap the rhythm displayed on the card. Other ideas include a relay game, where two teams of students compete to be the first to correctly dictate or clap back all the rhythm patterns. Joy Morin offers some free resources to get you started with rhythm activities for your students (https://colorinmypiano.com/category/rhythm/).

Melody Matchup

Create a set of flash cards of short excerpts or phrases from familiar songs and pieces. Then, cut each card into two or more parts—separating melodies from their lyrics or dividing phrases midline. Have students work individually or in pairs to match the correct halves together. This activity can be adapted for different skill levels by varying the complexity of the excerpts.

Create Your Own!

The games mentioned here are just a fraction of all the available piano and music games! Amy Chaplin of the *Piano Pantry* blog offers an exhaustive list of piano games and ideas at https://pianopantry.com/manipulatives-piano-games-private-group-lessons/. Let the fun keep flowing!

Technology

As digital natives, Gen Z and Gen Alpha students are used to and expect a certain level of technological integration in their daily lives. While there is evidence that digital saturation may have negative implications, the reality is technology is here to stay. Using digital tools for the sake of embedding technology in your studio is not a good strategy. However, integrating apps, software, and devices that streamline business practices, enhance learning environments, and simplify pedagogical tasks can significantly boost productivity, foster deeper student engagement, and free up valuable time for more meaningful instruction. Furthermore, many music-related apps intended for instruction are games. They incorporate many of the gamification characteristics discussed earlier. See table 9.1 for a list of the valuable tools we have encountered through our own teaching and conversations with other instructors. Other suggestions are also provided for customizing lessons and inspiring students.

Of course, there are and will be many more apps and programs that will prove helpful in your lessons and classes. Make a habit to continually search for and explore new educational apps. A Google search, brief ChatGPT conversation, or scan of the App Store or Google Play Store can shed light on up and coming tools to further your lesson goals.

Furthermore, children and teenagers love it when they can show something new to their teachers and parents. Young people have knowledge too, and they want to share it! The most obvious area where they usually have greater insight is technology. By asking students for some help and explanation with technology related to the piano lesson, teachers can build a layer of trust and interdependence. They may also be able to find some interesting music-related apps themselves!

Backing Tracks

While this form of media can be considered a type of technology, backing tracks deserve their own category. These amazing little recordings can serve as a whole orchestra that backs up a student and can make them feel like a star pianist. Many of the popular methods, like Piano Adventures, Hal Leonard's Piano Lessons, and Alfred's Group Piano for Adults, already offer backing tracks for their pieces. Students can often access them with a code that accompanies the book or through the method book's website. It is important to use these tracks, especially at the early stages of playing the piano. Beginners may feel uninspired by the melodies in early method books, and these accompaniment tracks can really enhance the performance experience. Furthermore, they can help students maintain a steady pulse and also heighten their listening skills in order to play along accurately with the recordings.

This type of tool can be used beyond the method-book years, as well. Backing tracks have been a game changer for motivating late elementary and intermediate students to work on their technical patterns, like scales, chords, and arpeggios. There are apps that offer this experience. However, generic backing tracks can be found on YouTube, as well—just type in "backing track" along with the time signature, key, and tempo needed.

Table 9.1 Music Instructional Apps

Purpose	App	Availability	Description
Note reading	Note Rush	iOS and Android	Listens to students play notes on their instruments and provides instant feedback to improve speed, accuracy, and staff-to-keyboard association
Rhythm drills	Rhythm Swing	iOS	Helps students improve their rhythmic accuracy by tapping rhythms in time with a swinging monkey, offering immediate feedback and progressive challenges
Rhythm drills	Rhythm Lab	iOS	Offers customizable interactive exercises to develop rhythmic reading, timing, and performance accuracy through real-time feedback and progressive challenges
Rhythm drills	Rhythm Randomizer	Desktop and mobile	Generates rhythm exercises to practice rhythm reading with adjustable time signatures, note values, and playback features
Ear training and music theory	Perfect Ear	iOS and Android	Helps musicians of all levels improve their ear training, rhythm skills, and overall musicianship through lessons and drills
Note reading and music theory	PianoTheory.app	Desktop and mobile	Teaches and drills music-theory concepts using a virtual piano
Sight-reading and keyboard proficiency	Piano Marvel	iOS, Android, mobile, and desktop	Connects to a digital piano and provides real-time feedback on accuracy, rhythm, and timing; also contains sight-reading tests—a unique feature that evaluates and tracks sight-reading ability over time
Scales and chords	Piano Scales and Chords	iOS and Android	Helps users of all levels to explore chords, scales, and progressions through an interactive interface and visual tools; a useful reference to have on hand

Table 9.2 Backing-Track Resources

App	Availability	Description
iReal Pro	iOS, Mac, and Android	Provides more than fifty authentic accompaniment styles from jazz and Latin to pop, Afrobeat, rock, and reggae, featuring a variety of instrument options to play along with; comes with thousands of chord charts that users can play along with; includes the ability to create custom chord charts and backing tracks
Jamzone	iOS, Mac, and Android	Similar to iReal Pro but also includes lyrics in karaoke style
Drum Beats—Metronome	iOS	Plays drum patterns (no instruments) of different popular songs and allows customization of tempo
Online Drum Machine by Musicca	Desktop and mobile	Allows users to create their own custom drumbeat by placing different parts of a drum set, such as the bass drum and hi-hat, in different places; users can adjust tempo and save their patterns for future use by copying the link
Drumbit Online Drum Machine	Desktop and mobile	Similar to Musicca's Online Drum Machine; features twenty-one drumkits to choose from, including an Indian percussion collection and beatbox options; users can also save their patterns as .json files on their devices to upload onto the virtual machine
YouTube Backing Tracks	All devices	Contains a rich collection of drumbeat backing tracks in a variety of styles from disco to rock to tango; users can type "backing track ___ BPM, ___ time signature, ___ style" and select from a list of backing-track audios; also contains backing tracks for chord progressions and popular and jazz songs

Melody has produced numerous backing tracks for piano scales, arpeggios, and progressions, available on all major streaming platforms under the artist name MelMor94 (see textbox 9.2). Originally tailored for Florida State University's group-piano exams with key-specific albums, newer releases now offer full key coverage for broader use.

> **Textbox 9.2 Backing Tracks by MelMor94 for Scales, Arpeggios, and Progressions**
>
> **Spotify:** https://open.spotify.com/artist/7og0afdBgVpvlt7dEnkP5F
> **Apple Music:** https://music.apple.com/us/artist/melmor94/1702372789
> **YouTube:** https://youtube.com/channel/UCMpXn_MOTqNZc6BWEWkU TaA?si=7pGET2l5uQM-whnj

Creating Your Own Backing Tracks

Did you know that you can create your own customized backing tracks for your students' pieces? First, analyze the harmonies of the piece that you want to create the track for, and then choose an appropriate tempo. From there, you can choose styles and instrumentation, but let's start with the basics. A great website to create a quick backing track is Musicca's Chord Player, an online platform that allows the user to select any chord quality for any duration, with options for easy saving and exporting (explained in more detail later in this chapter). More fun options for creating backing tracks include other online platforms, such as Soundtrap or BandLab (both explained in more detail later in this chapter). Both platforms offer more customization with MIDI connection options but also have smart-chord features that allow you to select chords without even touching a piano keyboard! Once you are satisfied with your backing track, export it and share it with your students.

Customizing Lessons for Your Students

Getting to Know Your Students

Offering piano lessons is not just a transactional relationship that offers an exchange of money for a service. To be an effective teacher requires one to understand the personality, strengths, and weaknesses of each student—and a piano teacher is no exception. Joe talked about the need to truly interact with students in a meaningful way. Often, the piano lesson is one of the few uninterrupted, individualized pockets of time a child has with an adult. Therefore, teachers need to take advantage of this opportunity and understand the impact they can have on these young lives. Whether a student comes to a lesson feeling particularly elated or gloomy, it is important for the teacher to always check in and know where the student is emotionally that day.

Gen Z and Alpha students are particularly in tune with their emotions and adept at recognizing and expressing what they are feeling.[1] Younger generations often feel that older individuals may not fully understand or empathize with their emotional experiences. However, these students are typically quite capable of identifying and expressing their feelings—especially when they feel safe, seen, and supported by their teacher. As a piano teacher, it's not necessary to reduce expectations or frequently assign less work when a student is having a tough day. Instead, small adjustments to the lesson's structure, pacing, or activities can go a long way in showing students that their emotional well-being matters. By responding with empathy and flexibility, teachers can build trust and foster a learning environment where students feel both emotionally supported and musically motivated.

Communicating with Students

In today's digital culture, emojis have become a surprisingly powerful tool for communication, with the 😂 emoji even earning the "Word of the Year" from Oxford Dictionaries.[2] Emojis have become the universal language of everyone who uses digital devices, and it is no surprise that Gen Z and Alpha students heavily use them. These visual symbols can convey tone, emotion, and feedback in a way that feels immediate and relatable. For piano teachers, using emojis in lesson notes, digital messages, practice charts, and even students' music can be an efficient and effective way to connect with students. A simple 😊 can signal a goal achieved, while a 💭 might encourage thoughtful practice. As emoji advocate Henry Kazinski, recently featured on the *New Yorker*'s Instagram account, boldly stated, "Emojis can do it all," arguing that they are far superior to traditional means of communication.[3] While that may be a stretch, there's no denying that emojis offer a playful yet meaningful way to engage students and reinforce learning in a language they instinctively understand. See figure 9.2 for an example of how emoji stickers were used in a student's piece to convey different moods.

Identifying and Broadening Musical Tastes

It is essential that we determine the types of music each of our students gravitate toward. This knowledge can inform the types of repertoire we include in their

Figure 9.2 Emojis on a student's piece to convey moods. *Photo by the author.*

curriculum plans. On the most simple and basic level, it can always be helpful to give students choice (or at least the illusion of choice) when selecting repertoire. Even when a range of options is offered, it is important that teachers are still sequencing skills in an optimal order and factoring in their overall pedagogical goals. For example, if a teacher notices that a student needs to improve their two-note slur articulation, then offering three pieces with different musical styles—but all featuring that articulation—and allowing the student to choose can help identify the type of music they naturally gravitate toward. However, we can and should go much further and deeper than this first step.

We can start by engaging in conversation with our students about their musical preferences. If they are willing, perhaps they can show us their Spotify or Apple Music accounts, and we can discuss the personalized recommendations the app chooses for them. Asking about their favorite movies and any video games they like to play will also offer some clues.

It may also be helpful to set up some type of online studio chat or group where students can share their favorite songs and pieces with each other to foster conversation about musical preferences. This could be as simple as a text, WhatsApp, a group chat on a social media platform like Instagram or Facebook Messenger, or the chat feature on an online studio platform. They will be encouraged to discuss why they like certain music and be exposed to other music they may not have encountered before. Teachers can glean from these conversations more information about their students' overall musical tastes and how they develop over time.

With digital streaming, YouTube, and other platforms, students have access to a plethora of musical selections. That means they are more exposed to music from around the world than ever before. Chapter 7 explains how Generations Z and Alpha are already primed to have open minds and ears

Table 9.3 Tools for Exposing Students to a Wide Range of Musical Styles

App	Availability	Description
Radiooooo	iOS, Android, and desktop	Billed as a music time machine; provides an interactive map where users can click on any country and any decade and then listen to the music that would have been enjoyed in that particular nation at that time in history
Bandcamp	iOS, Android, and desktop	Focuses on independent artists and labels; users can explore by genre, location, or what's trending
SoundCloud	Desktop and mobile	A hub for experimental and "underground" music; great for discovering niche genres, with artists often uploading remixes and original music
NTS Radio	iOS, Android, and desktop	Features shows hosted by DJs and musicians from around the world and numerous genres, from Afrobeat to Turkish pop
Spotify and Apple Music	iOS, Android, and desktop	Offer a vast variety of genres sorted by decade, region, and unique styles for countless hours of explorative and educational listening; Spotify's "Global X" and "world music" categories provide a rich and global variety of genres and styles; Apple Music provides interesting categories to explore, such as "Urbano Latino" and "Afrobeats"
Radio.garden	Desktop	Allows users to listen to live radio stations from around the world and to select any region they want from a 3D spinning globe
Accuradio	Desktop	Offers commercial-free world music online and a diverse mix of global sounds across multiple internet radio channels

about what they would like to listen to. We can take advantage of this mindset by placing in their hands tools that they can use to explore global music, expand their tastes, and find repertoire that speaks to them (see table 9.3).

Developing Coordination and Hand Strength, Improving Tactile Weaknesses

Chapter 5 discusses increasing evidence that some Gen Alpha students are demonstrating reduced hand strength and coordination. This can pose a challenge when tackling physical activities like playing the piano. It is crucial to find ways to help students overcome this particular difficulty. Here are some options.

Tracing Videos

These can help students enhance eye-hand coordination, along with developing how physical movement can synchronize with musical sound. The child watches the movements on the screen and then mimics the shapes by drawing on a piece of paper, tracing with their finger in the air, or following along with a scarf. A quick search on YouTube for "tracing videos" will offer a number of results (see textbox 9.3).

Using Objects

Because children conduct so much of their work and play on screens, they may not be used to picking up simple objects that previous generations got used to early in childhood. Squeezing items like tennis balls, stress balls, and Nerf balls that have different resistances can help children develop some of the smaller and unused muscles in their hands. Also, squeezing and using clothespins can assist with developing fine-motor skills.

Play-Doh

A staple for generations of children since the 1950s, this squishable, moldable compound still entrances youngsters today. While helping to strengthen the small muscles in their fingers, it also inspires imaginative play and creation. To incorporate this into piano study, Play-Doh can be used by students to create little notes that they place on a staff when learning about notation. Allowing their fingers to descend into the soft material can also give them a sense of what soft resistance is like and help them to be physically sensitive to the resistance they will feel when depressing keys on the piano.

> **Textbox 9.3 Doodling and Tracing Activity, Mozart Rondo alla Turca, Musical Song Map**
>
> A Different Musician, February 17, 2024, https://tinyurl.com/2hwj94xu

Small Toys

Developing the optimal hand position at the piano is essential for playing success (see figure 9.3). While each person's physiology is different, piano pedagogues can generally agree on what is a good hand shape. One of the most important aspects of this hand shape is that the bridge of the hand does not collapse when playing. If the hand stays in that position for a prolonged time, it can cause unnecessary strain and lead to eventual injury. To remind students of the optimal hand position, small toys can be used. Dr. Midori Koga at the University of Toronto came up with the ingenious idea of using dolphins. She found small, sand-filled dolphin toys that fit into the palm of a child's hand. The hand forms the shape of the dolphin, with the nose near the fingertips, the fin keeping the bridge (knuckles) upright, and the tail near the wrist. A "dolphin nudge" motion helps the student to understand the feeling of a portato touch. Imagine a dolphin gently nudging for food beneath the waves, with the keyboard representing the ocean or sea floor.

A short video clip of the dolphin nudge in action during a piano lesson is available at https://youtu.be/3Ql0pY-GgHU. The student is guided by the teacher to identify the different parts of the dolphin and associate them with the hand position. The teacher then helps the student to experience the fluid motion of the dolphin nudge away from the piano. Irina Gorin, author of the popular

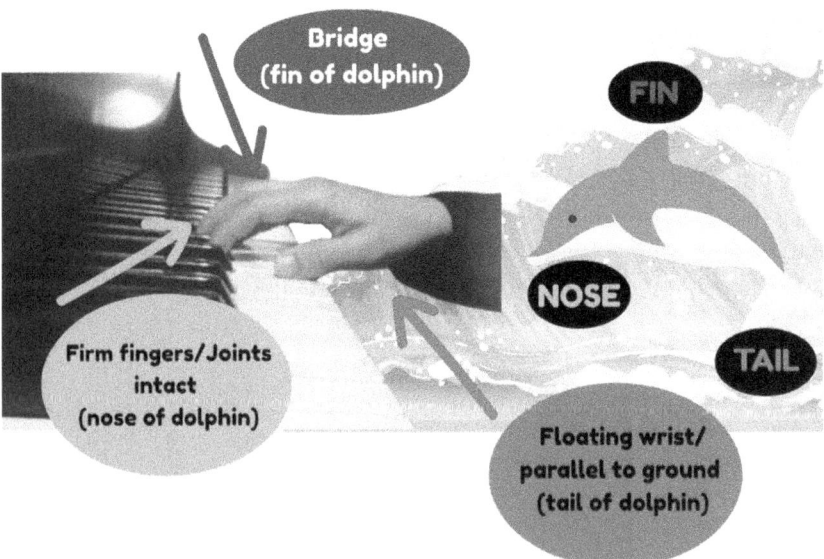

Figure 9.3 Proper hand position at the piano. *Illustration by the author.*

method book *Tales of a Musical Journey*, also uses toys and manipulatives, such as a smiley squeeze ball, mini noise putty, and long elastic bands for similar purposes. See her recommendations at https://www.irinagorin.com/collections/piano-lesson-toys. California teacher Diane Hidy uses ladybugs to encourage the same type of handshape (https://www.dianehidy.com/ladybug-lessons).

Creating Arrangements for Students

Arranging doesn't have to be difficult! If a student really wants to play a certain popular song or piece and it's either not accessible or too difficult for them to play, you can make a custom arrangement. First, select a notation software (see table 9.4). Second, use the best reference score that you can find to guide you as you create the arrangement. Analyzing the harmonies in the score (or on paper, if you do not have access to a score or chord chart) will prove very useful as you make your arrangement. Often, chords are

Table 9.4 Digital Tools for Compositions and Arrangements

Purpose	App/Website	Availability	Description
Composition, chord generator	Musicca Chord Player	Desktop and mobile	Provides chords of any quality that can be customized for duration of each chord and with twenty-five unique playing styles; users can save their musical creations and conveniently reload and share their tracks with a link
Composition, notation	Noteflight	Desktop and mobile	Allows users to create music and allows for layers of instruments; users can easily playback and export their composition as a PDF; similar to Sibelius and the now-extinct Finale program
Composition, notation	Musescore	Windows, macOS, and Linux	Similar to Noteflight; clean and intuitive interface; strong choice for creating scores and especially for sketching and learning
Composition, notation	Flat.io	Desktop and mobile	Similar to the previous Noteflight and Musescore; limited instruments and features on the free version but good for beginning students to use, as it has a simpler layout than other platforms

inverted and composed with patterns that contribute to increased difficulty. However, if you know the chord, just pop it in the score at the level you think is appropriate for the student (blocked and root position, blocked and inverted, broken, etc.). Then, the melody writing can begin! Again, melodies can be expanded with neighbor tones, arpeggiating patterns, and complex rhythms. So just like with the accompaniment, go ahead and pick out the main melody that makes the tune distinguishable, and adjust to the level of your student.

Inspiring Students to Engage in True Self-Expression

Once students have developed intrinsic motivation to practice and progress with their piano studies, and once their individual learning and emotional needs have been met, the safe space that is around them will blossom with their creativity. This is when they can be responsive to inspiration and truly communicate in an artistic fashion. Chapter 6 discusses the characteristics of creativity and explains how sometimes musicians get wrapped up in the thinking that only expert composers and improvisers can be creative. This is not the case. Creative thinking often begins with a small spark—a fresh perspective on a familiar idea or a subtle shift in approach. Even if the idea isn't novel to the world, it can still be original and meaningful to the person who conceived it. This section lays out a number of suggestions for fostering creativity and helping students express themselves through their music making.

Technology

The composition tools used in the previous section for creating student arrangements can also be introduced to your students for their own compositions and arrangements.

Group and Individual Activities

Draw What You Hear

Play different pieces, and have students draw pictures and shapes according to what they hear. For example, a piece with many staccato notes and more rough sounds may inspire dots on a page or something sharp. This will further develop the musical language and ways of thinking for students as they listen to music. It is always important to link what we're hearing to examples we can grasp and pictures that are easy to understand and explain to others.

Well-Rounded Listening

Play pieces from different musical eras, such as baroque, classical, romantic, impressionistic, and modern, and explain their musical characteristics while presenting art and architecture from the time to show how visual and musical art complement each other.

Improvisation

Forrest Kinney's Pattern Play and Create First! series are widely respected and innovative sets of books to help students of all ages and levels improvise at the piano. They include patterns for both ensemble and solo improvisations and can be learned by rote or by reading.

YouTube has a plethora of chord-progression videos that can serve as backing tracks. For example, a student can play an E-flat minor blues scale (all black keys plus A) with an E-flat minor twelve-bar blues video. This provides fun accompaniment and a sense of musical satisfaction because the students can feel as if they are playing with a band!

AI also can be a very useful tool. Using a picture generator like ChatGPT, CoPilot, or Gemini, you can create a scene either on your own or with your student and compose music based on the image.

Emojis are our modern-day hieroglyphics, and they have become widely used in communication and wordless expression among nearly everyone who texts. An improvisation activity can easily involve using emojis. Give a student one emoji or an assortment of emojis that tell a story, and use these to guide the mood of improvisation.

Multimodal Activities

Movement and Music

Kinesthetic Connections

Natalie Gilbert incorporated movement into her music curriculum and said that moving to musical rhythm is an involuntary, natural reaction. This teacher was creative with movement with music and used Haydn's third movement of Symphony no. 94, the "Surprise," to engage students in physical movement. They chanted, "Touch, touch, touch, touch, touch, touch, reach," while patting different parts of their body in quick succession and then reached skyward on the word *reach*. When the "surprise" occurred in the music, students made a large jump and froze, mimicking the dynamic change in the composition.[4]

Understanding Melodic Contour and Rhythm through Movement

Florida State University's pedagogy degree and certificate requires students to participate and teach in the children's practicum program. In this hands-on component, student teachers are matched with a young beginner-level student to whom they give thirty-minute lessons, in addition to accompanying them to the children's group class taught by the practicum supervisor. The one-to-one lessons and group classes include mostly rote teaching, with many singing and movement activities that take place off the bench. One such activity is the solfège ladder (see figure 9.4). This pedagogical strategy incorporates aural, kinesthetic, and visual learning modalities. Students can sing the solfège syllables of a major or minor scale while pointing to different parts on the body. They move from the toes (low "do") all the way to the top of the head (high "do") as they feel, hear, and see the upward motion of the scale. This can also be done backward to reflect a descending scale. This approach lends itself well to introducing steps and skips. Students can master the solfège ladder so that they can apply their knowledge for learning new melodies. A video of a student and teacher singing a version of the solfège ladder can be found at https://youtu.be/mAVyvlwVD-U.

Another playful routine frequently used is the Animal Actions Rhythm Game adapted from Sara Mullett's activity. Ms. Mullett's original plan is available at https://www.letsplaykidsmusic.com/animal-actions-rhythm-game/. FSU's practicum's version adapts rhythmic syllables inspired by Edwin Gordon's Music Learning Theory (MLT) to help students to enunciate and define different rhythmic patterns. It is important to note that a pure application of the MLT rhythmic syllables is not the goal for this activity. They are used to help students feel the macro- and microbeats within the context of 2/4 or 4/4 meter. While chanting the rhythms, students act out the motions of the animals. Table 9.5 outlines the rhythms most used from this activity.

Walking It Out

Another idea is to walk around the room while listening to a piece. Instruct students to take large steps when the music is loud and a gentler approach

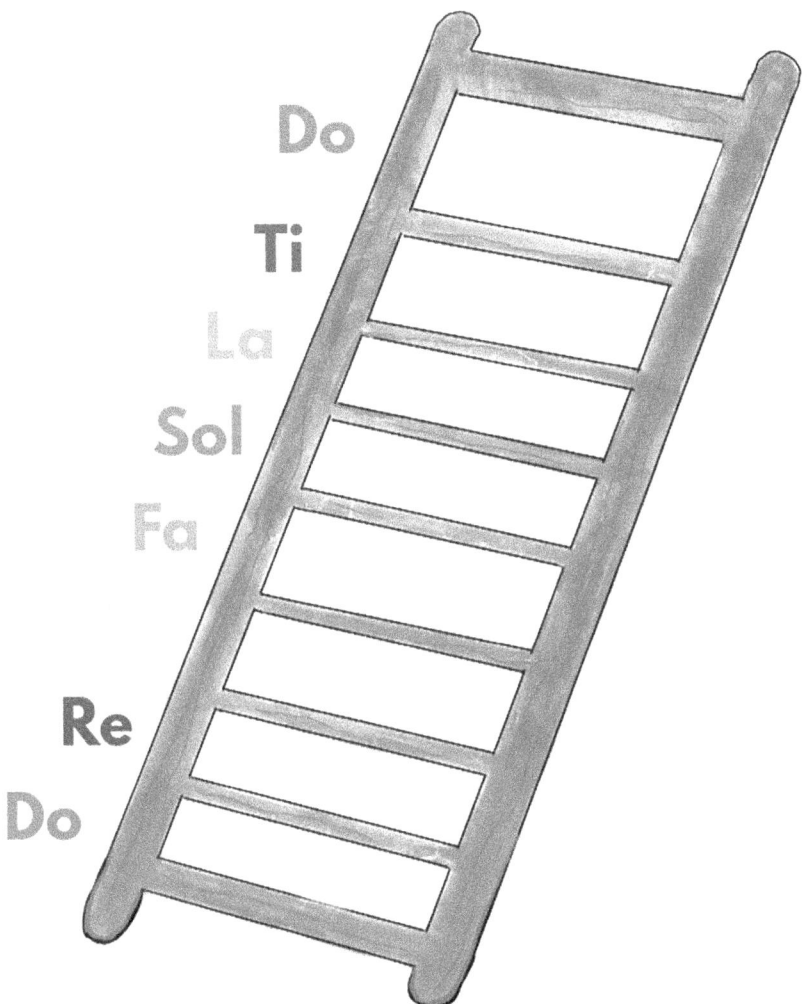

Figure 9.4 Do-re-mi ladder. *Illustration by the author.*

when the music is soft. In the same manner, if the music is fast, students can walk quickly and do the opposite for slower music. These concepts can be combined with the classic game of musical chairs, where students match their style of walking with the music's dynamics and tempo.

Props!

Friends of South Florida Music, a nonprofit organization that provides music education to schools that lack it, makes use of colorful scarves. In one of their

Table 9.5 Elements of Sara Mullett's Animal Actions Rhythm Game

Rhythmic Value	Animal/Movement	Rhythmic Solfège
♩ ♩ ♩ ♩	Elephant stomps (heavy stomps with alternating feet)	Du, Du, Du, Du
♩ ♩	Snail slides (drag each foot horizontally)	Du-u, Du-u (elongated *u* sound)
♫♫	Mouse scurries (jogging in place)	Du-ta-de-ta
♫ ♫	Penguin waddles (side-to-side waddles)	Du-de, Du-de
𝅝	Lion leaps (big jump and then resting)	Du-u-u-u (elongated *u* sound)

scarf activities, the teacher stays at the front of the classroom with a scarf in each hand. Each student also has a scarf in each hand and follows the teacher's movements while keeping time with the music's tempo. A video of this activity can be found at https://www.youtube.com/watch?v=HWNhTOh5JEE.

Visual Arts and Music

ArpieMaster

In the app *ArpieMaster*, multiple tapping triggers several balls to play the same tone at staggered intervals, creating layered rhythmic effects. The interface features a row of boxes arranged like a keyboard, with lower pitches on the left and higher pitches on the right.

Graphic Design Software

Canva and Adobe Express can help students create a collage or idea board of a piece. See figure 9.5 for an example.

Illustrated Score

Invite students to create a narrative or imaginative story that pairs with the piece they are learning. Once the story is developed, ask them to illustrate key moments or "chapters" of the story directly onto their sheet music. These

Figure 9.5 Idea board for Chopin's Nocturne in E Minor. *Created by the author.*

illustrations can be small drawings, symbols, or even color-coded markings that represent different moods, characters, and scenes.

Another option could be using AI to create pictures and cartoons that depict the different emotions of a piece. Such apps as Meta.AI, ChatGPT, and DALL-E create vivid representations based on the prompts the user inputs. For example, the teacher and student could enter "A smiling farmer working on his land with happy animals and surrounded by a beautiful landscape with sunshine and puffy clouds." The resulting picture could inspire a student who is playing "The Happy Farmer" by Robert Schumann.

This creative approach helps students connect emotionally with the music, deepens their interpretive understanding, and makes practice more engaging. It also encourages them to think about phrasing, dynamics, and tone in a more personal and expressive way, transforming the score into a visual and musical journey.

Literature

Selecting a piece from a historical era or geographical region that a student is currently exploring—whether in school or through personal interest—

can deepen their understanding and bring the music to life. This contextual approach helps students see music not just as sound but also as a reflection of culture, time, and place.

Encourage students to create a narrative that pairs with their piece, dividing it into chapters that align with the musical structure. This storytelling process enhances their interpretive skills and emotional connection to the music. For shorter works or pieces with fewer contrasting sections, writing a poem can be a powerful alternative. It links the literary and musical parts of the brain, fostering creativity and a more holistic artistic experience.

Examples to inspire poems include the following:

- **Franz Liszt:** Liszt is credited with developing the symphonic poem, a single-movement orchestral work often inspired by literature or other nonmusical sources. His symphonic poems, such as "Les Préludes," were influenced by poetry.
- **Richard Strauss:** Building on Liszt's foundation, Strauss created several famous tone poems (a term he preferred for symphonic poems) based on literary works, such as "Don Quixote" and "Thus Spoke Zarathustra."
- **Claude Debussy:** Debussy's orchestral work "Prélude à l'après-midi d'un faune" was inspired by Stéphane Mallarmé's poem of the same name.
- **Ralph Vaughan Williams:** Vaughan Williams's "The Lark Ascending" is a musical response to George Meredith's poem.

On a smaller scale, having a list of words that can be used for different sections of pieces is also a good idea (e.g., *bold*, *daring*, *furious*, *wide*, *heavy*, *triumphant*, and *relentless* for forte sections).

Composition

Composition is more approachable for both teachers and students than many think. Encourage students to constantly explore sounds they like on the piano. Implementing a sound-exploration segment into lessons for early years can prevent students from becoming hesitant with experimenting with different combinations of keys. One idea to keep this going is to assign students to create a short melody (optionally with accompaniment) based on a picture, mood, or even emoji, as shown in figure 9.6. From here, students can learn about basic chord progressions and start including a melody limited to chord tones at the start. The more you and your students practice creating

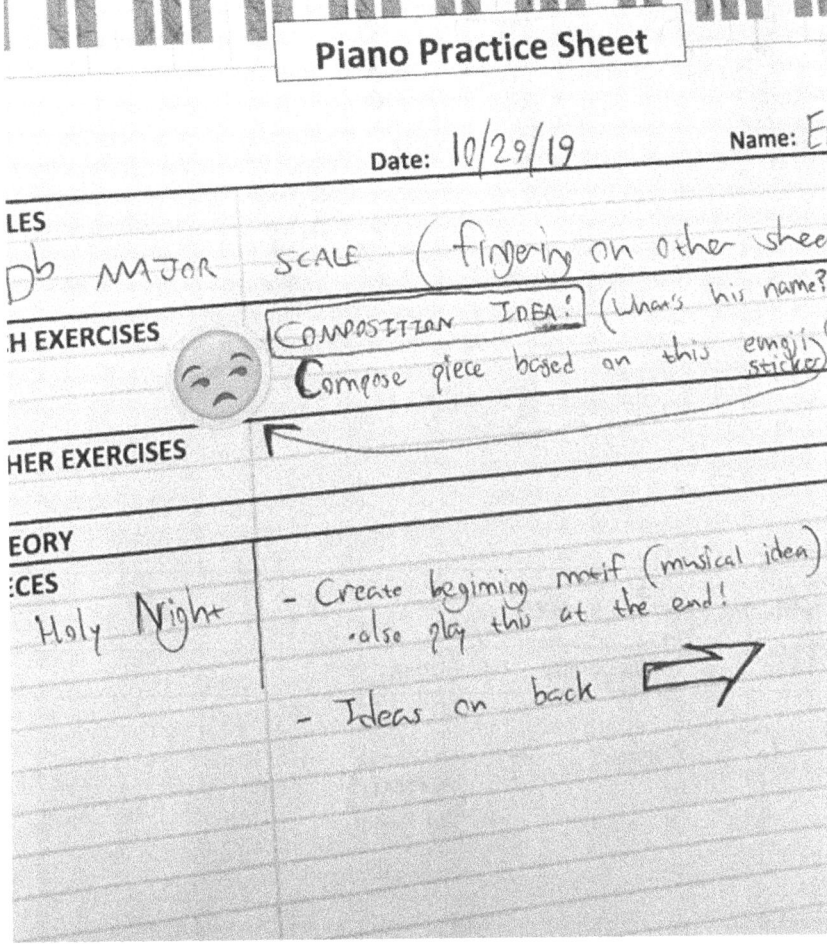

Figure 9.6 Composing based on emojis. *Created by the author.*

your own music, the easier it will become! Table 9.6 presents digital tools that can get younger students with little to no musical background started with compositional activities. For music notation, check out the table.

Digital audio workstations (DAW) are great spaces for students to experiment with layers, sounds, and beats (see table 9.7). Users can either click on the onscreen keyboard and chord tools or plug in a digital keyboard to a computer, tablet, or smartphone via a USB-B–to–USB-A cord (see figure 9.7) to use the MIDI interface (USB-A adapter needed for mobile devices). Check your digital keyboard to make sure that it contains a USB-B input (often labeled as MIDI or USB).

Table 9.6 Compositional Tools for Young Students

Purpose	App	Availability	Description
Composition, exploration	Sketch-A-Song	iOS and Android	An excellent way to introduce composition to young students just starting to dabble in music creation; knowledge of notation is not required; students choose a preset harmonic "sketchpad" to create a multilayered composition; users notate their music through color and can choose from a variety of timbres and voices; preset grooves are also available
Composition, exploration	Chrome Music Lab	Desktop and mobile	Lets users create short musical compositions using a grid interface; designed to be intuitive and visual; requires no prior music-theory knowledge and is great for beginning students

Table 9.7 DAW-Inspired Tools

App	Availability	Description
Soundtrap	Desktop and mobile	Free online platform students can use directly from desktop or mobile view or connect to a keyboard via a MIDI cord to input sounds; preset drumbeats, a variety of instruments, and manual drumkit sounds are available to play from computer keyboard or digital piano keyboard
BandLab	iOS, Android, and desktop	Similar to Soundtrap; lets users create music via desktop/mobile device with or without digital keyboard connection; provides a collection of instruments and a setting called "Smart Chords" that allows the user to play different chords with one click; drum kits can be used from either a computer keyboard or a digital piano keyboard
Garageband	iOS	Provides a streamlined interface and a wide range of built-in instruments, loops, and recording features, making it accessible for beginners while still offering creative flexibility; users can record live instruments, including piano, or use virtual keyboards and MIDI input to compose music; a strong entry-level tool for learning the basics of music production, composition, and audio editing

Figure 9.7 USB-B–to–USB-A cord. *Illustration by the author.*

This list of strategies only scratches the surface of the innovative endeavors you can use to stimulate your students' interest in piano study and help them to spark new ideas and connections. The last couple of decades have provided us with new technologies and progressive ways of thinking. By combining these approaches with the timeless fundamentals of sound pedagogy, artistic intent, an open mind, and a student-centered approach, we can ensure piano playing is an activity that young people will want to explore and excel in for years to come.

Notes

1 "The Empathy Revolution: Navigating Gen Z Emotions in the Workplace," Talking Talent, 2024, https://talking-talent.com/us/insights/latest-thinking/the-empathy-revolution-navigating-gen-z-emotions-in-the-workplace/.

2   "Word of the Year 2015," Oxford Languages, accessed October 19, 2025, https://languages.oup.com/word-of-the-year/2015/.
3   Dan Rosen and Sam Bronowski, *Free Yourself from Literacy, with Emojis* (*New Yorker*, January 6, 2022), https://www.newyorker.com/humor/daily-shouts/free-yourself-from-literacy-with-emojis.
4   Natalie Gilbert, "Music and Moving," *American Music Teacher* 44, no. 6 (June/July 1995): 18, https://www.jstor.org/stable/43542827.

Index

Page numbers in italics refer to figures and tables.

adaptability
    Gen Alpha strengths, 64, 70, 71
    teaching strategies, 86, 136
AI. *See artificial intelligence*
Alpha, Generation. *See Generation Alpha*
American Music Teacher (journal)
    1940s–1990s educational media mentions, 11–13
    articles, two-part millennium series, 1
    columns, Computer Connection, 14, *15*
    radio and industry notices, historical, 12, 14, *15*
anime, 124–6
anxiety, 46–8. *See also mental health*
Apple products and services, 44, 59. *See also Technology*
arrangements, 124–6, 135–8, 146, 161–2
artificial intelligence (AI)
    ChatGPT, 60–1, 76, 83
    CoPilot, 48
    DALL-E, 61, 167
    deep learning, 60
    evolution of technology, 17–20
    Gemini, 61, 163
    Generation Alpha technology, 60–2
    Generation Z usage, 83–5
    Meta AI, 61, 167
artistry
    expressive interpretation, 105
    melodic contour, 164
assessment
    Florida State Music Teachers Association (FSMTA) Student Day, 10
    Guild Auditions, 10
    Royal Conservatory of Music, 10, 126
    Student Events and Assessment, 9
attention span
    gamification, 108
    Gen Z characteristics, 48, 50, 51–2
    Gen Alpha characteristics, 59, 66
audio-visual teaching (historical)
    film (1940s initiatives; MTNA Visual Aids), 11–12
    television/satellite instruction (1950s–1970s), VHS 2–3
authority, 50–2, 87–8.
awareness
    global issues, 91–2, 147
    musical, 105, 120
    physical, 107, 137

baby boomers, 31–3
Bach, C.P.E.
    Essay on the True Art of Playing Keyboard Instruments (1762), 2
backing tracks
    early media (records, tapes, cassettes), 12
    modern use in studio (YouTube drum patterns, accompaniment, for improvisation), 80, 92, 108, 128, 152–5, 163
BandLab. *See Digital Audio Workstations (DAW)*
baroque (era, piano pedagogy)
    finger action emphasis; treatises (Diruta, Couperin, Rameau), 2–3
    improvisation/ornamentation, figured bass, 2–3, 99
Beck, Martha, 102, 128

Canva, 146, 166
challenges
    of Generation Z, 51–2
    of Generation Alpha, 66–9
    of Generation Z piano students, 75–80
    of Generation Alpha piano students, 87–91
Chat GPT. *See artificial intelligence*
Chee-Hwa Tan, 129–31
chiroplast (Logier device), 2–4
Clark, Frances, 8. *See also method books*
classical (era, pedagogy), 2, 18, 99, 120, 124, 148
coding, 58–9, 84
collaboration
    Generation Z social life, 49
    motivating your piano students, 145–6
    piano studio example, 124–6
communication
    Generation Z, 48–50
    Generation Alpha, 66, 88
    radio and recorded sound, 12
    teacher-student, 117–19, 156
composers, 18, 82, 130, 142–3, 162
composition
    as a vehicle for creativity 100–2, 104
    historical ebb and revival 18, 99–100
    multimodal triggers (images, stories, movement) 105–7, 140–1, 163, 168–9
    student choice, creative outlet 142–4
    technology 107–8, *161*, 169–70
computers, 14, 34, 44, 80
coordination, 158–61
COVID-19
    online education, 18, 47–9, 82, 146
    influential event, 45, 63, 87, 123, 128, 133
creativity
    fostering creativity, 99–111
    piano studio examples, 127–31, 140–1
    in self-expression, 162–3
Csikszentmihalyi, Mihaly (flow), 6, 101, 108–9
culture, 18, 114–15, 147–9
curiosity, 58, 64–6, 88, 102–3, 128–9, 142
customization
    of backing tracks, 154–5
    of lessons, 65, 132, 135
Czerny, Carl, 3

DALL-E. *See artificial intelligence*
Dalcroze, Émile (eurhythmics)
    integration into early-20th-century pedagogy, 8–9
    movement linkage, 106–7
Danyew, Ashley, 141–4
development
    of piano teaching (Russia, Europe), 2–5
    of piano teaching (United States), 6–9
    professional, 9
    psychological, 67
    social, 51, 69
digital
    devices, 10, 57, 156
    digital age, 14. *See also Technology*
    digital collaboration, 146
    digital ensemble, 146
    digital intelligence, 92
    literacy, 58–9, 69–70, 92
digital audio workstations (DAW)
    BandLab, 107, 155, *170*
    GarageBand, 107, *170*
    Soundtrap, 107, 155, *170*
Disney
    repertoire, 124
    streaming, 61
distractions, 46, 81, 88
diversity, 48, 52, 58–9, 116–17, 141, 148
dolphin nudge, 160
drawing, 105–6, 131, 159

education
    baby boomers, 32
    Generation Alpha
        gamification; personalization; adaptive/AI-enhanced expectations; need for parental support; social/attention challenges, 64–6, 67–9
    Generation X, 35
    Generation Z
        multimodal/hybrid comfort; self-reliance from pandemic; shorter attention spans; instant-result bias, 47–50, 51–3

G.I. (Greatest) Generation, 29
millennials, 38
Silent Generation, 30
emotions
   emotional awareness, 58
   emotional expression, 50, 105–6
   emotional development, 63
   emotional growth/skills, 66
   emotional intelligence, 87, 92
   emotional response, 67, 69, 81
   in music making, 118–119, 130–1, 156, 162, 167–8
English school, 6

Facebook
   Facebook groups, 18, 89
   Facebook usage, 33, 49, 79, 83, 157
family, 29, 31–2, 34, 60, 63–4, 87. *See also parents*
feedback
   in pedagogy, 10, 118, 156
   technology-based, 14, 17, 79, 152
   through gamification, 109
flexibility
   adjusting expectations, 138–40
   in learning, 47, 50
Florida State University, 154, 164
formative events
   baby boomers, 31–2
   Cold War, 34
   COVID-19, 63, 87
   definition of generation, 25
   Generation Alpha, 57–8
   Generation X, 34
   Generation Y (millennials), 35–7
   Generation Z, 45
   Great Depression, 28
   Great Recession, 36, 45
   G.I. (Greatest) Generation, 28
   hippie movement, 30, 32
   September 11 attacks, 35, 44
   Silent Generation, 30
   stock market crash, 28, 34
   Vietnam War, 32
   World War Two (WWII), 28–9
French school, 4, 6

G.I. (Greatest) Generation, 28–9
gamification, 64–5, 77–80. *See also games*

definition and learning design; motivation and flow, 108–10
GarageBand. *See Digital Audio Workstations (DAW)*
Gemini. *See artificial intelligence*
generation
   definition, 25–6
   importance of generations, 26–8
   overview of generations, 28–39
Generation Alpha
   attention span, visual learning bias 13, 54, 56–7, 61, 65, 72, 96, 114
   challenges, 66–9, 76-8
   demographics, 57–8
   family dynamics, 63–4
   education, 64–6, 76–7
   influential events, 62–3
   parental involvement, 63–4, 66
   strengths, 69–71, 80–1
   technology immersion, 57–8, 59–62, 67–8
Generation Y. *See millennials*
Generation Z
   attention span and instant results, 43–56
   challenges, 51–2
   cultural awareness, 52–3
   education, 47–8, 50
   global connectivity, 52–3
   influential events, 44–6
   mental health, 46–7
   social communication preferences, 49, 50
   strengths, 52–3
   technology use, 43–4
   workforce characteristics, 49–50, 51
Gordon, Edwin, 107, 164
group classes/group culture, 132–5, 164

Harkins, Joe, 135–9
history
   of piano pedagogy, 2–10
   of technology, 10–17
   used in piano pedagogy, 125–6, 148
holistic, 17–18, 99, 102–3, 168
Hisaishi, Joe (anime/Studio Ghibli)
   repertoire appeal and stylistic bridges to Chopin and impressionism, 124–5

identity
  music as self-expression, 102–4
  musical tastes, 113–14
imagination, 19, 100, 107, 131
improvisation,
  history, 2, 18
  in piano lessons, 99–100, 102, 104, 108, 163
independence
  finger independence, 6. *See also technique*
  in the music studio, 108–9, 143–4
influencer, 60, 62, 66, 69
informance, 141–4
innovation, 11, 28, 37–8, 126, 144
Instagram
  general usage, 37–8, 44, 49, 57, 61–2, 79
  educational usage, 47, 82, 157
instant gratification, 48, 51–2, 77
intelligence
  digital, 69, 92
  emotional, 87–8

jazz, 99, 105, 124, 136, 138, 154

Kalkbrenner, Friedrich, 3
kinesthetic, 104, 129, 163–4. *See also movement*
Kodály, Zoltán, 107

Lazarus, Penny, 123–26
leadership, 38, 50, 89, 135, 140, 143
learning
  active learning, 70
  aural learning, 129
  deep learning, 60
  kinesthetic learning, 129
  machine learning, 83
  movement-based learning, 144
  multimodal learning, 50, 105–110, 164
  online learning, 16, 18, 47, 63, 64–6, 82
  outcomes, 117–19
  peer learning, 141
  personalized learning, 65, 80–3, 102–4, 129 162
  preferences, 47–8, 50–3, 64–6, 70–1
  project-based learning, 123–6, 149
  rote learning, 137–8

self-directed learning, 144
visual learning, 77–80, 90–1
Lee, Marie, 132–5
Leschetizky, Theodor, 5
lesson activities, 99, 102, 104–10
lesson design and structure, 117–20, 126, 128–9, 144, 156
listening
  active listening, 88
  audio streaming platforms, 16, 44, 85, 117, 120
  imaginative listening, 102
  listening activities, 102, 105–6, 119–20, 136, 142, 162–6
  listening tools, 152, 158
  playlists, 78–9, 119–20
Liszt, Franz, 3–4, 168
literature, 167–8
Logier, Johann Bernard, 3. *See also chiroplast*
Long, Marguerite, 6. *See also method books*
low-tech approach, 142

master class, 3–4
Matthay, Tobias, 6
mental health
  anxiety, 46–8, 51, 81, 102–4, 127–9
  depression, 46, 48, 51, 67
  early emotional development, 63–5, 87
  screen time and well-being, 43–71
Meta AI. *See artificial intelligence*
method books
  Mayron Cole Group Piano method, 132
  publications, 8, 12
  reading approaches, 8–9
  repertoire, 137, 152
millennials (Generation Y), 35–9
Minecraft, 62, 108, 136
motivation
  autonomy, 81–3, 89, 118, 124, 128–9, 130
  creativity as motivator, 99–111
  external motivation, 9
  in games, 64, 149–51
  in groups, 133
  loss of, 80
  responsibility, 133
  self expression, 162

student choice, 138
technology, 65
movement
   as means of musical expression, 106–7, 127, 130, 139–40, 142, 159, 163–5, *166*
   motor abilities/skills, 67–8, 71, 90, 159
   political, 30–2, 46, 63, 125
multi-sensory approach, 129, 139
multitasking, 80
musical preferences
   general, 127, 136, 142, 145
   complexity and familiarity (Hedgehog; Inverted-U); exposure and authority effects, 113–20
   Gen Z/Alpha streaming habits; eclectic tastes; lyrical content concerns, 116–17
musical tastes
   broadening, 156–8
   exposure, 119–20
   influences, 113–17
Music Learning Theory, 107, 164. *See also Gordon, Edwin*
Music Teachers National Association (MTNA), 1, 9, 106, 134

National Conference on Keyboard Pedagogy (NCKP), 9, 134
Neuhaus, Heinrich, 5
non-verbal behavior, 119
nostalgia, 36, 116

Orff, Carl, 8, 107, 139

Pace, Robert, 8. *See also method books*
painting 105–6
parents
   of G.I. (Greatest) Generation, 28
   of baby boomers, 32
   of Generation X, 34
   of Generation Y (millennials), 36–7
   of Generation Z, 45
   of Generation Alpha, 38, 63–4, 66, 68, 69–70, 87–9
   gentle parenting, 38
   parental involvement, 66, 89
   in piano lessons, 132–44, 147, 149

pedagogical games and tools
   analog games, 28, 35–6, 85
   backing tracks, 108, 152, 154–5
   composing with emojis, 156
   computer games, 14–15, 69
   DAW-inspired tools, 169–70
   games, 145–71
   music ensembles, 146
   in music lessons
      Create Your Own!, 151
      floor staff, 150
      Jeopardy, 150
      Melody Matchup, 151
      music bingo, 150
      music instructional apps, 153–4
      music trivia, 150
      note-word-spelling competitions, 150
      online gaming, 62, 64
      progress map, 77–8
      rhythm-dictation games, 151
      solfège ladder, 164
      tracing video, 159
peer
   influence, 114
   learning, 141
   pressure, 134
Philipp, Isidor, 6. *See also method books*
physical motion, 130. *See also movement*
piano pedagogy
   historical development, 1–10
   transformative pedagogy, 118
piano team, 133, 135. *See also group classes*
piano technique, 130–1. *See also technique*
piano schools (historic), *See Russian school, French school, English school*
play
   toys and games, 59, 62, 64, 67, 69, 160–1
   imaginative play, 105
   Play-Doh, 159
   playing games in pedagogy, 108. *See also gamification; pedagogical games and tools*
   ribbon play, 140
Plazas, Pilar, 13–14
postural deficiencies, 90. *See also technique*

practice
- check-in videos/weeklong guidance, 77
- teaching practices, 2–10
- parental role and accountability. *See parents*
- piano practice strategies, 77–8, 133–9, 140, 143–4, 147, 156
- piano practice discussion, 89, 118
- practice expectations, 143
- *Practice Space*, 127, 134
- progress maps, 77–8

professional association, 18. *See also Music Teachers National Association, National Conference on Keyboard Pedagogy*

professional development, 9, 134

project-based studio and learning
- themes, organization, strategies, 12, 36, 147–9

radio, 12, 30, 85

recording
- technologies, 17, 92, *170*
- videos, 85, 146–47

repertoire
- adapting to students, 145–72
- choice, 105
- creative use, 145–172customization, 136
- drawbacks, 99
- emotions, 130
- expanding the canon, 18, 113–22, 124
- historical trends, 1–24
- in groups, 133
- musical preferences, 117
- personal taste, 114–17, 141, 156–8
- project-based selections, 147–9
- student-selected music, 105, 120, 124–6, 128
- understanding the background, 142–3. *See also Informance*

Richardson, Nathan, 7

romantic (era, pedagogy), 3, 163

rote learning, 137–8. *See also learning*

Russian school, 5

screen time, 51, 59, 68–9, 70, 87, 90

self-directed learning. *See Learning*

self-expression, 104, 107, 141, 145–6

September 11 attacks. *See Generation Z influential events*

Silent Generation, 30–1

smartphones, 16, 44, 60, 80

social media, 16, 18, 37, 44, 83, 157. *See also Instagram; Facebook; TikTok; YouTube*

social development
- effects of pandemic, 46–7, 49, 51, 63
- effects of technology, 59, 62, 67–8, 87
- social skills, 49, 51, 59, 63, 68

songwriting, 104. *See also composition*

Soundtrap. *See Digital Audio Workstations (DAW)*

Spotify, 16, 44, 117, 120, *155*, 157–8

stereotypes
- dangers of overgeneralization, 25–42
- generalizations, 27

storytelling, 117, 131, 140–1, 149, 168

streaming services
- audio, 16, 44, 117, 120, 154, 157
- video, 44, 57, *61*, 85, 147

studio
- communication, 88
- environment, 126, 144
- group classes, 132–5
- management
- organization tools, 127–9
- pedagogical strategies, 145–72
- physical set up, 137
- projected-based studio, 123–6
- technology for organization, 127–9

Tan, Chee-Hwa, 129–31

teaching
- case studies, 123–44
- history of teaching practices, 2–10
- rote teaching, 107. *See also rote learning*
- strategies, 145–72
- trends, 17–18
- technology, 19–20, 86, 93

teaching technologies, historical
- predigital age (film, printing, radio, TV, electronic instruments), 11–23, *13*, 14
- digital/personal-computer age (Apple/IBM school pilots, CD-ROM,

178 Index

Computer Connection), 14–15, *15*
internet age (MP3, streaming, YouTube, smartphones/tablets), 15–16
artificial intelligence age (public release, adoption, risks/benefits), 17
technique
    arpeggios
        technique and expressive function, 130–1
        practice with backing tracks and DAW-style tool, 152–5
    finger action
        Baroque and early methods, 2
    mid-19th century etudes, 3–4
    hand shape, 8, 160. *See also dolphin nudge*
    hand strength, 68, 158
    historical approaches, 2–10
    mindfulness technique, 81
    pianistic technique, 130–1
    portato touch, 160
    postural deficiencies, 90
    stress balls, 159
    tactile weakness, 158
technology
    AirPods, 59
    apps, *153–4*
    Among Us, 62
    Apple Music. *See Apple Products and Services*
    Apple Watch. *See Apple Products and Services*
    artificial. *See artificial intelligence*
    Augmented Reality, 91
    backing tracks, 152, 154–5. *See also Backing tracks*
    ChatGPT. *See artificial intelligence*
    CD-ROM, 14
    composition and technology, 107–8, 161, 168–71
    DALL-E. *See artificial intelligence*
    DAW (Digital Audio Workstation), 169, *170*
    developments in technology, 10–17
    digital devices, 10, 59
    digital intelligence, 92
    digital natives, 44

Facetime. *See Apple Products and Services*
film, 11
floppy disk, 14
Fortnite, 62
Gemini. *See artificial intelligence*
Generation Z, 43–7, 52–3, 83–5
Generation Alpha, 59–62, 64, 68–70, 85–6
electronic instruments, 13
emojis, 156
iPad. *See Apple Products and Services*
iPhone. *See Apple Products and Services*
internet, 15–16
in education, 19, 78–9, 102–4, 151
JavaScript, 59
MP3, 15–16
Meta AI. *See artificial intelligence*
Minecraft, 62
Open Broadcasting Service (OBS), 147
online gaming, 62
OpenShot, 146
online studio chat, 157
Open Broadcaster Software (OBS), 147
personal computers, 14
Python, 59
Roblox, 62, 66, 108
Shotcut, 146
Skype, 44
social media, 16, 18, 37, 44, 83, 157
smartphones, 16, 44, 60, 80
Spotify, 16. *See also Spotify*
studio case studies, 127–9, 135–8
streaming services, 16, 44. *See also Streaming*
technology-based feedback, 79
television, 12
Tenuto, 79
texting, 59, 79–80, 83
TikTok, 37–8. *See also TikTok*
video editing, 146
video game music, 136
virtual music ensembles, 146–7
virtual reality (VR), 59, 91
Windows Live Messenger, 44
YouTube
    creation of YouTube, 16, 44
    Generation Alpha usage, 67

Index   179

technology *(continued)*
    Generation Z usage, 48, 50, 60–1, 76, 82, 91
    in education, 7, 16, 19
    streaming, 44
    tutorials, 7, 19, 136, 138
    use in the piano studio, 152, *154–5*, 157, 159, 163, 166
    as a teaching tool
        backing tracks, 108, 152, 154–5
        examples, 135–8, 141
        demonstration videos, 79
        hand-eye coordination, 159
        listening, 120, 157
        improvisation, 163
        rhythm games, 166
Thompson, John, 8, 12. *See also Method books*

TikTok
    educational usage, 47–8, 50, 82
    general usage, 37–8, 43, 60–1, 67, 79, 87
trust, 66, 117–18, 138, 140, 152, 156

video editing, 146. *See also technology: Open Broadcaster Software (OBS); Openshot; Shotcut*
Viss, Leila, 127–9
visual arts, 105, 166
visual learning, 77, 90, 91, 164

work-life balance, 49–50

YouTube. *See technology*

Z, Generation. *See Generation Z*